KIDS, COMPUTERS & YOU

WHAT PARENTS CAN DO NOW TO PREPARE THEIR CHILDREN FOR THE FUTURE

Frank B. Edwards
&
Thomas H. Carpenter

BUNGALO BOOKS

Bungalo
Books

For Debi and Susan, our favourite teachers

Written by Frank B. Edwards and Thomas H. Carpenter
Cartoons and cover illustration by John Bianchi
© Copyright 1995 by Bungalo Books

Canadian Cataloguing in Publication Data

Edwards, Frank B., 1952-
    Kids, computers & you : what parents can do now to
    prepare their children for the future

ISBN 0-921285-39-6 (bound)   ISBN 0-921285-38-8 (pbk.)

1. Education—Data processing.   2. Computers and children.
I. Carpenter, Thomas, 1959-.   II. Title.   III. Title: Kids, computers
and you.

LB1028.5.E39   1995   371.3'34   C95-900126-3

Published in Canada by: Printed in Canada by:
Bungalo Books   Friesen Printers
Suite 100   Altona, Manitoba
17 Elk Court   R0G 0B0
Kingston, Ontario
K7M 7A4

Distributed in Canada by:
Firefly Books Ltd.
250 Sparks Avenue
Willowdale, Ontario
M2H 2S4

TABLE OF CONTENTS

Introduction	5
Preface	9
Kids and the Classroom	25
Schools and the Information Highway	69
Teachers	93
The Administration	119
The Home Front	145
Conclusions	153
Acknowledgments	160

INTRODUCTION

Computers are not typewriters. That is the first truth, and the second is that no one yet knows exactly how best to use computers, especially in schools. People, including teachers and everyone else associated with computers in the classroom, need to be constantly reminded that keyboards and monitors are not just roundabout ways of putting words on paper. It is true that studies have indicated students work longer and more creatively when pen and paper are replaced with a word processor, where changes are simple and painless. But word processing is only a small part of the power that a desktop computer can bring to a person, and keyboarding is just one of a series of skills that we should want our children to acquire.

Futurist author George Gilder, a senior fellow at Seattle's Discovery Institute, draws a wonderful parallel between the computer and the automobile.

Imagine, he tells audiences, that you are an Amazonian native with no knowledge of modern technology, and you stumble across a brand-new car in a clearing. The key is in the ignition, and as you approach it, you feel the heat from its idling engine. Climbing inside, you discover that its instrument panel can bring you music. Fire can be summoned at the push of a cigarette lighter. Depending on your needs, the car can warm you or cool you. The seats are comfortable for sitting or sleeping. Its roof keeps the rain off your head, and the trunk provides excellent storage for your belongings. You can have light at night, use the horn to scare away dangerous animals and even keep track of time with a digital clock.

An object with this many practical functions would no doubt attract a lot of excitement and perhaps even become the focus of an entire village. But until the natives found someone to put it on a highway and show them how it moves, they would never know its real power or the function for which it was designed. Any debates they had about using the machine would be incomplete at best.

The same can be said of the computer. The people who are just now discovering it for their own use — often for word processing and amusement — are largely missing out on its greater potential as a communication device capable of moving information and sharing ideas. Given the number of typewriters in use a decade ago, it is not surprising that computers first found their way onto office desks as replacements for typewriters, but that role is changing radically.

The fact that ordinary people can also manipulate data and create digital models of real objects seems to have escaped many users. With the addition of extra programs (the software that gives shape and meaning to the computer hardware's raw processing power), a typist can also create two-dimensional art, cartoon animation, simulations of flight, games or scientific experiments, family budgets and even data bases filled with information about family members or customers. And, with the use of a few cables and some peripheral devices, that information can be sent to inexpensive printers to be put onto paper (a format that we seem to be most comfortable with) or even onto telephone lines, where it can be shared, in a matter of minutes, with other people around the globe.

In these days of headlines and high-powered talk about the Information Superhighway, the computer is being hyped as a communication device that will allow anyone to broadcast his or her own digital creations to the rest of the world while browsing the creative talents of everyone else. Although the advocates' superlatives should be taken with a grain of salt, these declarations about the power of the computer deserve serious attention. We are certainly entering a period of incredible change that is being driven by a generation of computers which are relatively inexpensive and, by the standards of the sixties and seventies, incredibly powerful.

So, having accepted that computers are changing the world and our lives, we have to ask, "What should our children be doing with computers?"

What is the place of computers in our schools? Are computers about to become android teachers that work for free and never lose their patience? Or are classrooms best left out of the computer revolution so that our kids can get on with the task of learning without the distraction of dubious games which are more entertainment than education? Should we, in fact, be loading our kids up with computer equipment at home so that they will be better prepared for the future?

And, perhaps most important, what will the outcome of the policies of the nineties be 20 years from now? Will we have created a well-trained generation of efficient communicators who use computers to serve their needs? Or will there be a technological divide through the middle of society with those who were fortunate enough to acquire technical knowledge on one side as a new privileged class and, on the other, the majority who were not given access to the power of technology?

Right now, it is much too soon to say.

PREFACE

Nine parents out of ten insist that kids must receive computer training in school. But if you ask them why, they stumble. "The workplace of tomorrow," they may say, "demands that children acquire computer skills if they are to earn a living in a changing world. That's all there is to it."

Others may suggest that "this is the age of information, and everyone, especially students, must be linked up to the information highway." Few will have a complete explanation, but almost all will continue to applaud as the momentum for technological change grows stronger, even if it means that meaningful debate and thoughtful planning are pushed aside by panic decision making.

There are plenty of reasons for the panic: newspapers overflow with articles about the coming information-based economy; the new corporate wealth of the eighties was produced either by tiny chip-driven gadgets or new pieces of software; governments are stressing computer training for the jobless; and businesses are replacing workers with machines. Not surprisingly, parents want their children to be fluent in the new language of success. And practically everyone assumes that computers in schools are undoubtedly already a priority for most school boards.

Despite people's strong conviction that computers have a place in schools, most parents have little or no idea how well computer technology has been integrated into the classroom. People do not know what hardware is in place or what software their children use; they do not know what pedagogical theories guide decisions being made by school boards and teachers; and in general, they have no means of judging the success of the current system or even of determining whether anything meaningful is going on at all.

That's what this book is about.

Do we need computers in schools? What are they for?

How do parents find out what is going on? Can they help?

These questions deal with the practical matter of how our kids spend their days in school and what they get out of it. Trying to answer them is a dizzying process, and it is little wonder that parents have more determination than information. Things are changing fast.

The Ballpoint Pen Revolution

When I was in grade five, in 1962, the revolutionary new mass-market technology was the ballpoint pen, and I wanted one. In our classroom, whether it was a school-wide policy or merely the whim of an eccentric teacher, we used straight pens. There we sat each day, under the stern tutelage of our Mr. Jackson, learning to write the old-fashioned way. Every few minutes, we paused to recharge the long, fragile nibs with ink from the small pots recessed into the right front corner of our desks. And with every dip and every tedious pen stroke, I got a little more ink on my fingers.

A messy writer at best, I was constantly frustrated by the blotches on my notebooks. On the worst day of that year, Mr. Jackson, a teacher I had regarded with a healthy mix of fear and respect, held up my science notes for all the class to see and suggested that perhaps I had dipped the claws of a dying chicken into my inkwell and let it perform its death dance upon my page. The humiliation was as senseless as the technological issue that inspired it.

No doubt those teachers who, like Mr. Jackson, clung to the old-fashioned pen nib had their reasons. Perhaps they were motivated only by the fact that all our desks still had circular holes cut out for inkwells. Whatever the reasons, it took years before all kids benefited from the wider variety of writing tools available to us in the mid-20th century, and hindsight says there was no good reason for the delay.

It is no surprise, then, that I react badly, and perhaps somewhat personally, today when I hear of teachers who do not allow students to use computers to prepare essays. A common rationale seems to be that a computer-generated script looks too slick and can somehow disguise faulty scholarship. Better by far, say some, to slave over a handwritten treatise than to whip one up on a word processor that allows constant revision and correction.

Luckily, my 11-year-old son is blessed with an open-minded teacher who actually encourages word processing. A reluctant essayist, Scott can be cajoled into decent work, but like his father, he prefers one-draft efforts if he can get away with them. Recently, he prepared an assignment on the North-West Rebellion in the 1880s. While his first draft was the correct length, I noted that it had a few shortcomings.

"Young man, I guarantee that you'll never succeed with such sloppy handwriting."

He resisted making the necessary changes, arguing that he would have to rewrite the whole piece, but I dragged him to my old computer and gave him a quick lesson in two-finger typing. Within an hour, he had punched the piece into place, corrected the spelling with the help of the gentle beep-beep of a spell-checker program and inserted the necessary corrections and changes into the essay, concentrating on the parts that needed revision rather than having to rewrite the entire few pages over several times.

When he left for school the next morning, he carried the assignment with him proudly — printed out on spotless white paper by a laser printer that produces professional-looking type regardless of the age or inclinations of the user. He got a B+ for his efforts, but more important, he ended up with an essay that looked worthy of his efforts. No doubt, his teacher found it easier to concentrate on the meaning of the words rather than the neatness of the handwriting. I suspect that neither of them felt the computer had altered the essence of this traditional educational activity, and in a couple of obvious ways, the process and product were enhanced.

Scott's shift into the academic use of computers and word processing did not end with his essay. A few days later, he pecked the first draft of a book report directly into the computer, editing and revising as he wrote. Not only did he produce a better assignment this time, he also saved himself the pain of transcribing a handwritten draft into a word processing program. Like everyone else in grade six across Canada, he had read the book that he reported on and gathered his thoughts on the meaning of the book, its characters, its setting and its messages, but when he set off to write down his ideas, he used a keyboard and computer screen instead of paper and pen. Mistakes cleaned up neatly with simple keystrokes that left no holes in paper, no smudges, no eraser tailings. No frustration.

Again, the academic function of the assignment — the reading, the analysis, the writing — had been preserved and only the final presentation changed, and the 30 minutes or so that Scott saved by not having to *copy his work out in good* (that phrase continues to haunt me even 30 years after I left public school) probably got frittered away doing something he considered more important than his book report. No doubt, as he flipped through the channels on television, he figured that he had beaten the system.

There is also a slim chance that he realized he had put an amazing technology to work for him.

Computers: Yes, No, Yes, No...

For adults with a limited exposure to computers, and even for those who use them every day in the workplace, the debate over technology in the classroom can seem to be a confusing one, and most people are not clear about where the commotion arises. It is easy to assume that there is a master plan at work. After all, if technology is bounding ahead so quickly and if our daily lives are being filled with automatic bank tellers, electronic telephone-call handling, voice mail and cars with solid-state everything, a parent can be forgiven for assuming that these advances are finding their way into the school system. But is this so?

Surprisingly, few schools in Canada seem to have a workable computer policy in place. Effective computer use in a classroom is more likely to be the result of an enterprising teacher than a master plan. And official school board policy is as likely to get in the way as it is to help.

Young Scott's first foray into practical word processing is a good example. He was fortunate that his teacher allowed assignments to be prepared on computer. There are teachers who still argue that having to learn how to master the keyboard detracts from the actual assignment, and others forbid it because students with computers at home have an unfair advantage over those who do not. A few, uninitiated in the ways of computers, simply ban their use, because they do not understand the implications of using a machine to prepare an assignment. Caution often dictates that a classroom moratorium be imposed on the unknown.

In the staff rooms of the world, these issues are being hotly debated — usually without input from parents or students. So, too, in school board meetings where similar well-intentioned debates about how best to realize the promise of the new technology get mixed into the pot with flinty-eyed concerns about the tax base.

And while groups of computer-literate educators discuss the immensely complicated (and very sexy) question of how schools can exploit the resources of the coming Information Superhighway, other teachers and administrators are still arguing about the proper grade level at which to introduce keyboarding skills — the most basic use of computers. If the debate were about air travel, the first group would be discussing the value of international destinations while the rest would be arguing over seating arrangements on the plane.

The fact that something as basic as keyboarding attracts so much heated debate shows how confounding the issues are. Some schools introduce primary-grade children to keyboards while they are still learning the alphabet. Others have declared that only by grade six are a student's hands big enough to be able to handle the rigours of touch-typing. Some high schools are still resisting the trend to earlier keyboard mastery, arguing hollowly that keyboarding (a direct descendant of our old grade nine typing classes) should remain a high school credit course. Meanwhile, 5-year-olds with computers at home are teaching themselves to type so that they can play their favourite games.

Unfortunately, in many schools, the debate about keyboarding is about as far as the technological-philosophy debate goes, as if word processing were the only practical use for a computer. This emphasis on keyboarding no doubt reflects the fact that all teachers and administrators have a basic high school typing (or keyboarding) class in common and therefore find it an easy debate to understand and to join. In the meantime, the broader issues still go unnoticed, and day-to-day computer use is left in the hands of individual teachers.

Swept Up by the Computer Boom

In 1991, I gave up a career in magazine and book publishing to join a friend in running a children's book-publishing business that we had started earlier as a part-time enterprise. Bungalo Books was outgrowing its moonlighting roots, and we had to give it serious attention.

It is important to realize that only 10 years earlier, quitting my job and starting my own company would have been incautious at best and probably completely impossible. Publishing back then required a production staff and at least $100,000 worth of typesetting equipment, but we were able to start out with a single $15,000 computer system that allowed us to do all the work ourselves.

The same machine that became our entire production staff also served as a word processor, a bookkeeper, a correspondence secretary and, in conjunction with a temperamental answering machine, a digital go-fer. Whirring away on my desk, the computer represented the equivalent of four or five part-time staff. Without realizing it at the time, we had become part of the small-business computer phenomenon that allowed two people to do the job of several others.

A year later, my partner moved 6,000 kilometres away to Arizona to broaden our horizons in the United States, and we found ourselves relying on computers and an online telecommunications service for our daily contact with one another. Without really planning to, we had followed our computers into the age of commuting to work by telephone and computer. It was about this time, as I was coming to appreciate more fully the extent to which computers had entered and changed my workday, that I innocently asked my children what they were learning about computers at school. Their answers gave me my first glimpse into the Pandora's box of computers and education in the nineties.

As I consciously assessed my own children's experience with computers, I was astounded by the discrepancies in their computer use. Our youngest two had acquired a completely different attitude toward computers than their older sister, who regarded the machines with disdain.

Our teenage daughter had completed a year of keyboarding in grade nine, but that seemed to be the limit of her exposure and, predictably, the limit of her enthusiasm for computers. The younger two, in grades one and four at the time, said that there were computers in their classrooms, but they had never used them. The teachers seemed indifferent to them, and they were usually not working properly anyway. They preferred to use the old Apple Macintosh I kept at home. Even though it was black and white, it was easy to run. Curious, I asked the principal about the school situation. She explained that there were old computers in each of the classrooms but that the school's best unit was kept in the library, where it was hooked up to a CD-ROM which gave kids access to one copy of an electronic encyclopædia.

A quick survey of the school convinced me that the equipment was antiquated junk and had frustrated the teachers to the point where they refused to use it as a serious part of their curriculum.

During a meeting with the teacher who was supposed to act as the staff expert on this pitiable collection of machines, I learned that he felt it was all quite useless and that he had abandoned any pretence of keeping it running. When I asked for a demonstration of the system at work, he explained that the school had been without the use of the computers for a couple of weeks and that they were awaiting the arrival of a school board technician. To meet the standards set out by the Ontario government in the early eighties, the computers were strung in a network so that they could all share the same software, but like a string of cheap Christmas lights, when one part of the chain blew, nothing else would work. He guessed that the school computers were unavailable to students half of the year because of breakdowns. Not surprisingly, he hated the things and preferred to talk about his own home computer, a Macintosh that has a reputation for easy use and relative dependability — especially for computer novices.

Although I knew little about the uses of computers in school, it struck me as ludicrous that our school could be so poorly served. Assuming that budget restrictions were keeping good equipment out of the school, I went to the parental advisory committee and asked the members to consider using its budget to buy new computers. But there was little enthusiasm for the idea. The group's short list of worthy projects included a sun shelter, new flowerbeds, gymnasium equipment and a three-day campout, but no one seemed interested in putting money into computers. The teachers and principal, with no real experience using computers in the classroom, were not ready to encourage the purchase, and the parents were lukewarm on the idea.

Fired up with the enthusiasm of a new convert, I attended the parental advisory committee's next meeting with a proposal for a mobile desktop publishing system that would allow students to create their own books, newsletters and posters. Attached to a decent printer, it would allow kids to incorporate art, photographs and words into any project they chose. I had shopped around for the best prices, had figured out an educational link that was bound to create some interest and had chosen the perfect model — the same kind I used every day at work. It was the graphics industry's standard machine and was easy to use in situations where people hated reading manuals.

Sensing a spark of interest, I asked that my new proposal be put to a vote but listened with dismay as the chairperson fretted aloud about rushing into a project of this size. Perhaps, she suggested, I could arrange for representatives of both Apple and IBM to come to our small school to do a sales pitch before the committee decided on spending the $3,000. I knew I was truly finished when the principal pointed out that school board policy probably would not allow the donation of nonstandard equipment anyway. I left the meeting dejected.

The Bucks Stop Here

The next stop in my computer crusade was the administration offices of the local Board of Education. I asked to be placed, as a community representative, on a committee that was reassessing the use of computers and multimedia equipment within the rural Board's 21 schools. I joined a superintendent, two principals, several teachers, the director of computer services and three technicians.

Within an hour of the start of my first committee meeting, it became clear that with two exceptions, the educational half of the group really did not have any experience with computers — in or out of the classroom. Policy seemed to be dictated by the technical staff, whose job was to keep the Board's equipment running even though they, like me, had little idea of the educational issues involved in computing.

Oddly, much of the first meeting was concerned with television rather than computers. Teachers wanted to switch officially from Beta to VHS format VCRs. It seemed that while parent groups were donating the more common VHS format equipment to schools, the video libraries contained Beta tapes that could be played only on the Board's ageing (and ailing) machines. The debate raged on for over an hour before a technician explained his reluctance to switch. Someone at the Board office had bought hundreds of Beta format blank tapes on sale the previous year (a few thousand dollars' worth), and the technical department was reluctant to stop buying expensive Beta equipment until the tapes were used up. By ignoring a technical trend that had swept North America, the fellows in tech services had stalled an inevitable change for years, increasing the Board's investment in overpriced equipment instead of cutting its losses early.

It was to become a common theme in the Board's computer deliberations.

Getting up my courage, I decided to ride the momentum of this new spirit of change and introduce the idea of switching to better-quality computer equipment. Pointing out that the ICON computers which were found in most classrooms were outdated and hard to maintain, I suggested that they be officially declared redundant so that all new equipment be either IBM- or Apple-based technology.

Reasons for the status quo came raining down on me. The Board's software was mainly ICON-based. The reputation of the Apple brand of equipment had been marred by its early computers. The technicians could not be expected to maintain different brands of equipment. They knew the ICONs well and were comfortable with IBM equipment. The teachers were not trying hard enough to learn to use the equipment they had. There was not enough money, and computers were a low priority.

I attended monthly meetings with these people for half a year, and they proved how tough it is to implement change in any education system. Their information and theories were often half-baked or completely erroneous, and although the rest of North America was struggling with

"I'm glad we decided to spend more time playing with the computer."

these very same issues, our local people felt completely alone and unprepared for their task. I watched as they set about reinventing a wheel that was being reconstructed a thousand different ways by a thousand different local bureaucracies. They never seemed to equate the power of technology with their day-to-day lives or their jobs or the education of their children.

They also seemed to think that they were powerless to change any part of the administration which had set the rules 10 years before, and that was basically that.

Adjusting the Status Quo

By now, I had approached the problem at every level available to a parent. I had talked with other parents; I had talked with teachers and principals and school board employees and elected representatives. I had served on committees and helped generate detailed proposals for change. In the end, however, nothing happened. The Board of Education governing my children's schools was not ready to pursue the implementation of the next generation of microcomputers in schools. What's more, the members generally seemed to feel that the first experiments with computers, those that had taken place over the past 10 years or so, were a complete failure.

Employees of the Board of Education did not feel pressure from elected representatives to change how things were done; elected representatives were not feeling pressure from voters or from parents for change, probably because too few people knew what was at stake. And those few who did had little chance of being heard.

My own misadventures spawned the idea behind this book and in some ways dictated its approach. The lessons that we offer here involve a rudimentary understanding of the decision-making processes that drive school policies. Most parents, including myself, have much to learn about affecting change in schools, but there are some basic approaches that one can take at the Board level, at the school level and in the classroom. And even at home where, after all, kids spend most of their time.

Our ambition is not to join debates or to argue points of view. Rather, we hope to create a reference map with which parents can locate themselves and their own situations. Hopefully, after a few hours with this book, parents can work toward their own conclusions about the potential that computers offer their kids and how best to exploit it.

Frank B. Edwards
February 1995

KIDS AND THE CLASSROOM

Computers in classrooms have been a fact of life for more than 10 years now, and although their integration into day-to-day school life has not been particularly smooth or easy, it is safe to say that computers are definitely in schools to stay.

What has made their existence a bit harder to accept is the fact that they haven't really replaced any other piece of traditional equipment. While those noisy 16mm film projectors and old-style filmstrip projectors disappeared with the advent of VCRs and television sets, the computer arrived by itself, without much history behind it. Unfortunately for teachers and students in those early years, the classroom computer was still very much a work-in-progress, and its early configurations were complicated, confusing, difficult and sometimes downright impossible to figure out. After all, the companies that designed them had originally aimed for business customers, and not a great deal of attention had been paid to the education market before.

Even so, a lot of people began to imagine the impact that computers could have on education, and there was a ground swell of support for the new technology. In Canada, hundreds of thousands of computers were shipped to schools by provincial governments — but the initial interest and enthusiasm gave way to despair when people plugged the stuff in. The teachers were not usually ready for computer technology, there were limited places to slip it into the curriculum, and the electronic boxes seemed stubbornly incapable of living up to their revolutionary billing. They were designed to be run by people who loved to talk computer-talk.

If it had taken administrators an extra decade to jump onto the computer bandwagon, then life with a classroom computer might be much easier today. The equipment would be cheaper, faster and easier to use; the adult community of parents and teachers would have had time to adjust their attitudes toward technology and education; and there would probably be so much desire to catch up to the computer trend that by now is all around us in business and at home, it would have been an easy transition to make.

Instead, computers entered the classroom in fits and starts. Over half of the existing machines now in schools are obsolete junk that more often than not drives the teachers who have tried to use it away in frustration. Having invested millions in the old stuff, school boards have no money left to buy the recent generations of computers that could deliver on the educational promise of the information age.

Parents stepping into the classroom to investigate the situation and try to find solutions may be met with hostility, disbelief or, perhaps, a weary welcome by teachers who hope that help is finally on the way.

What Are Computers Doing in School Classrooms?
Depending on the teacher and the school, that computer at the back of the classroom could be a dynamic link in your child's learning process. Or it could be an expensive electronic box that is taking up space which would be put to better educational use by a cage of gerbils. Parents need to know what computers are good for, they need to know how they are actually being used in their children's classes, and they need to keep track of new uses that come along.

Parents also need to preserve a healthy skepticism, especially in the face of some of the popular metaphors about computers in schools.

Many who support the idea of computers in schools say that the modern microcomputer should be like the pencil, a ubiquitous tool which is readily available to all schoolchildren. Simplifying a complex argument, they suggest that kids and teachers casually use pencils every day without fretting about how they work or how they fit into educational programs, so why not treat computers the same way? Just as you toss a pencil into your desk or tuck it behind your ear until you need it, keep lots of computers at the ready all the time. Make them as familiar and comfortable for children as the simplest technology of today. That way, children will be prepared for tomorrow.

Unfortunately, the uses of computers are not as well

defined in the modern scheme of things as pencils are.

Reversing the comparison highlights the problems: what if pencils really were like computers? Imagine that every month or two for the foreseeable future, someone created yet another use for pencils: stacking them like building blocks, using them as counters in elementary arithmetic lessons, tossing them in games, using them to send signals.

"I told you it was only a matter of time before we were replaced by a computer."

With each new use, pencil manufacturers would release yet another new model, complete with a new set of users' manuals and a very attractive price. With every passing month, the value of old pencils would drop, even though they were still capable of doing the job for which they were originally purchased. Even worse, each new use would attract a group of loud supporters arguing that they alone had apprehended the true nature of pencils and had found the ultimate place for pencils in our society.

Of course, everyone already knows what pencils are really for, and most of us are confident that their role is not likely to change. Computers, on the other hand, are evolving faster than people can follow, and parents who want to track the changes and their influence on schooling need to avoid all suggestions that computers are comparable to anything as simple as a pencil. We do know a few things, however, and those include the fact that computers are already a combination of blackboard, notebook, textbook, telephone, fax machine, art board and, yes, pencil.

How Are Computers Being Used in Classrooms Now?
Despite some confusion and debate over how computers should be used in schools, a few broad categories of use have emerged and stayed — while others have come and faded away.

For now, experts generally agree on five basic uses for computers in education:

1. They provide word processing (typing).
2. They can analyze and manipulate data.

3. They can interact with a user to simulate real events and play games.

4. They can present information.

5. They can communicate with other computers, allowing distant users to share information.

Word processing, as we have already said, is one of the most common uses of the computer in schools, especially in high school and senior public school. Word processing courses replaced typing classes a long time ago (an obvious fact to anyone who has tried to buy an electric typewriter or browsed secondhand shops recently), and the age at which kids now start typing is falling dramatically. Some schools are even offering keyboarding classes to grade five and six students with the notion that youngsters want to type their assignments anyway, so why not teach them how to use all 10 fingers early on. It is a reasonable argument that, if adopted widely, will finally bump grade nine keyboarding classes out of existence, much to the chagrin of those who insist that it has always been and should remain a high school subject.

Certainly, it makes sense to teach these skills earlier so that during their school career, students can take more advantage of the speed and flexibility which word processing offers. By retarding the development of such a basic skill for too long, educators are hindering an efficient use of equipment that is already available in public schools and are forcing kids to develop bad typing habits which will be much harder to break when they do finally hit the officially sanctioned grade for learning the skill.

Lowering the grade at which keyboarding is introduced

will require some province-wide curriculum changes, but it is probably possible to start offering mandatory courses as early as grade five or six, catching the students who are in grade seven and eight during the transition period as they go into grade nine. Of course, children who can demonstrate typing proficiency when they do enter high school (perhaps because they learned how to type properly at home or in public school) should be exempted from the agony of a high school typing course. High school keyboarding could be replaced by courses that teach basic desktop publishing skills and English composition or any other subject which would allow students to apply their technical finger wizardry to more useful intellectual pursuits. As we go deeper into this new information age, all students should be required to become proficient at keyboarding, with an increased emphasis on practical communication skills.

But Won't Keyboards Soon Be Obsolete?
Although it would be foolish to dismiss the notion of voice recognition totally, it seems improbable that keyboards will disappear entirely — at least for a very long time. Dictating to a machine is unlikely to be much more efficient than typing one's own words directly. Good typists should be able to compose words on a keyboard, driving their fingers to keep up with the speed of their thoughts. It is an innate skill that reporters and authors seem to develop naturally, far removed from the copying habit that we learned in school (do a rough draft by hand, then type it out in good), and it really is not a hard one to develop. Every cub reporter

for the past century has had to learn it on his or her first few days on the job, and as word processing has gained respectability, more and more skilled workers and senior administrators have taken it up — especially as company typing pools have shrunk.

Basic speech recognition became a staple on many personal computers in 1994, a few years after Apple began to install built-in microphones on all of its computers. These machines can now be set to respond to specific voice commands, such as "Open File/Close File," and can read back typed words, so indeed, they are not far from being able to take dictation.

But technology is not always as practical as it first appears. It is safe to assume that talking to a computer may be fine in a private office or at home, but it will not work in other environments. Libraries and classrooms full of students dictating notes and assignments would produce a noisy buzz that would preclude serious academic pursuits, and office situations would be just as distracting. Further, it might be proved that the speed of fingers on a keyboard is better matched to thoughtful communication than the speed of a flapping tongue. Certainly, when a dictation session is completed, most users will still prefer making corrections and changes to their correspondence with the aid of a keyboard and a moose rather than clumsily describing the location of errors to the computer. (Oops. "Computer, go up. There. Turn left. Go back six words. Change that spelling from m-o-o-s-e to m-o-u-s-e. Done.")

*　　　*　　　*

Data manipulation is another major use of computers in classrooms. Like word processing, its origins are directly tied to business — the data processing business, to be exact. The first use of computers was to crunch numbers, taking scientific data and formulas and rendering them meaningful in a shorter time than human beings could calculate them. Census data, astronomical measurements, voting patterns and testing of new mathematical theories have all been handled by computers, because computers work quickly and accurately and can sort huge amounts of information into countless categories. Universities and then business enthusiastically embraced the science of data processing after the Second World War and built a dense layer of mystique around it. Until the personal computers of the early eighties appeared, with word processing and simple data processing functions, the world of computing was far removed from ordinary life.

In the sixties and seventies, few of us considered a career in the computing industry. In our minds, high school computer nerds became programmers and data analysts, while less ambitious graduates learned the trade of the data processor, simply entering information into whatever language or format a computer needed in order to do its magic. High school business departments offered training for the latter, leaving the black art of programming to universities and colleges.

But with the arrival of computers in the schools of the eighties came a wave of educational programs that at first taught basic data processing skills to senior students but then filtered them down into the earlier grades. Today, spreadsheets that allow users to perform tasks both straightforward (bank-account balancing) and complex (financial cash-flow projections) have been simplified to make them accessible to everyone. Instead of teaching data processing as a subject on its own, science and math teachers now use computers as tools that can demonstrate the relationship between theoretical formulas and real statistics.

Even primary-grade teachers have students enter such comparative data as weight, height or age into a spreadsheet to show the relationship between individuals and groups. Abstract equations can take on a new meaning as they are used to manipulate information that is meaningful to students.

Neil Armitage, a grade seven teacher on British Columbia's tiny Saltspring Island, teaches the use of spreadsheets to his students as part of their regular science curriculum and finds that kids accept and use the programs as readily as they use pocket calculators. But he and his colleagues are an exception, not just because they know how to run the programs (which are now part of the standard fare that comes with most new inexpensive computers) but because they have managed to tuck technical training into the background of regular science courses. "I assume that when kids arrive in my class, they know the basics of this stuff," he says. "But those coming in from other districts come up short."

*   *   *

Computer *simulations* of real-life experiences have been the main focus of most of the software that has found its way into the classroom in the past 10 years. The most primitive programs were simple flashcard exercises in which students sat in front of screens while numbers flashed before them. If "one plus one" appeared, the student would type two, get a visual reward, then await the next question. The theories behind this style of drill work grew out of a long teaching tradition that brought us our memorized knowledge of the alphabet and the multiplication tables. Refinements have turned the exercises into games. Children can work their way through mazes, answering math or spelling questions at each step, being rewarded with access to secret rooms of imaginary castles if they give enough correct answers.

More advanced programs followed as software developers learned the benefits of adding colour, sound, animation and high-quality graphics to their packages. By turning lessons into games, they invented the edutainment industry, which in theory mixes learning and pleasure in an irresistible blend. Simulations of exploration and settlement have been popular with history and geography teachers; primary-grade teachers often use programs that encourage reading and writing through following computer-generated commands.

One popular history simulation has students assuming the roles of settlers who choose resources from a limited inventory and then cope with the events that the computer concocts: blizzards, drought, bad neighbours, and so on. In high school, science teachers are discovering the value of synthetic experiments in chemistry and physics that allow students to mix chemicals or test natural laws without making a mess or endangering themselves.

*   *   *

"Multimedia," a catchword that is second only to "information highway" as a focus of today's computer industry, has revolutionized the computer's ability to *present information* in a form that encourages the user to interact with the machine. With the development of compact disk (CD) technology, which allows huge amounts of digital information to be placed onto a single disk, computers can now offer entire encyclopædias and multivolume reference works to users, enabling them to scan the equivalent of 100,000 pages of text for specific information. Flat text on a screen, of course, has limited appeal to kids and teachers alike, so software companies have gussied up their presentations with graphics, sound and even animation. Now a reference book can show film clips of famous speeches, colour photographs of animals and audio samples of birdcalls. Because of the nature of CD technology, access is almost instantaneous (depending on the speed of the machine), so there is no flipping through pages of books or viewing long segments of videotapes looking for specific information.

Not all information-presentation software is as sexy as the top-end products, though, and it is too soon to give up on books and libraries yet. The scholarship and imagination that has matured within the traditional book industry over the past 300 years does not exist in the software business. Pundits complain that current multimedia CDs are nothing more than sound-bite machines with little bits and pieces clipped from all over, then pasted together and cross-referenced. Certainly, though, multimedia presentations will prove a formidable teaching device if and when their content catches up with the technology.

*   *   *

With all the recent talk of information highways, the *communications* function of computers has taken the spotlight. Billed as an essential link that will connect people all around the world, the computer is being viewed as the ultimate telephone, a telecommunications device which can move words, pictures and sound back and forth over long distances instantly. Visionaries predict that it will change all aspects of our lives, not just education, and school administrators are racing to jump onto the bandwagon. Although the concept is still in its infancy, computer communications seems to be the driving force behind the new move to modernize technology within our schools, and parents should be aware of its newfound popularity.

But Isn't Computer Programming Important?

The computers of today are a lot friendlier than they used to be, and as a result, the once vigorous debate about whether kids need to understand programming in order to understand computers gradually washed away without ever being resolved. Computers are now so powerful that they can run intricate Graphic User Interfaces (GUIs) that virtually make the machines idiotproof. The complicated instruction codes that drive computers are hidden in the background by simple little pictures (known as icons), which shield users from the technical end of computing. Gutsy 3-year-olds and nervous adults alike can fire up a Macintosh computer after the briefest of introductions, and the rest of the world's computers are not far behind, as new, improved generations of Microsoft's Windows become available.

Simple personal computers no longer greet users with a blank screen when they are turned on. While the old DOS (disk operating system) common to most IBM-style computers required users to type complex numerical or letter commands to start work, the first thing you see when you turn on a machine today is a colourful display that lays out all your options on a simulated desktop. Word processing programs or games jump to life with a simple click of a mouse button. You don't need to know anything at all about computing; you simply begin clicking and typing.

This is not to suggest that the subject of (or the debate over) computer programming has disappeared entirely from schools. There are still those who insist that children should learn the basics of programming so that they can fully appreciate the powers and habits of the machines they use. Scholars such as Seymour Papert, author of the influential books *Mindstorms* and *The Thinking Machine* and creator of the programming language LOGO, also contend that learning to organize your thoughts in the ways that elementary programming demands is simply good for young minds.

The people who share Papert's general outlook believe that the ability to use computers and to control their functioning can tap deep into the human intellect. Simply mastering the logic of a computer language, according to this viewpoint, increases reasoning power and creativity, and for these people, learning the principles behind the machine is as important as actually using it. It is not a view that can simply be dismissed, especially since a great deal of what is taught in schools is valued as much for the mental exercise of learning as for the utilitarian end it serves. Just as a journey is more interesting than the final destination, the answer to a complicated math question or a history assignment is not usually as important as the thinking and research that were required to create it.

But Papert's critics warn about falling into the trap of teaching children to think like computers. While it may be an interesting exercise, the carefully logical, procedural "thinking" of the computer is far removed from the natural ability of children to reason. Instinctively, children see things as whole and feel their way around them rather than analytically stripping them down to their basic parts. In his very readable *The Cult of Information* (1986), historian Theodore Roszak warned LOGO enthusiasts that the programming world was too restrictive and that too many elementary school subjects (math, English, even art) were being linked to computer language:

"LOGO has a repertory [sic] of just so many colours, so many shapes....It is well suited to geometrical play but not to fantasy that oversteps those narrow boundaries....I found myself haunted by the image of the prisoner who has been granted complete freedom to roam the 'microworld' called jail: 'Stay inside the wall, follow the rules, and you can do whatever you want.' "

As well, programming requires large amounts of time that could be better spent. There is so much else to be done

with computers that limiting study to their inner workings
becomes increasingly pointless — like teaching timing-belt
adjustment to people who take Drivers' Education. For better or worse, the proponents of computer programming
or computer science have had to make lots of room for
those who want to close the hood and just learn to drive.
Computers now have so many other useful educational
applications that lessons in elementary programming and

*"I think they will clear up once you learn to type
with all ten fingers."*

binary code are a questionable use of both time and computers at the elementary level.

Parents whose young kids are being introduced to computer programming need not worry, as it certainly does teach thinking skills and a particular approach to problem solving. But if programming is the focus of the technology program, the school's computers may be in the hands of an ideologue — and an outdated ideologue at that.

Computer science makes more sense in high schools, where kids can learn about the hardware inside the box itself and about the chips that lie at the heart of every computer as well as programming. At this level, it is an option as valuable as the law or accounting or technical courses that prepare students for more advanced career training at post-secondary institutions. Computer science classes simply provide a way for kids to follow up their interest in the technology itself, and no one can question the wisdom of that.

How Did Computers Get Into Our Classrooms?

A lot of different types of computers have found their way into schools since the early eighties, when provincial governments began to buy the machines for every school. In the early days, the computers came from companies like Apple (Apple II) and Commodore (Commodore Vic and Commodore 64) that offered special models designed for schools and children. Sadly, many of those early computers remain in classrooms, limited to operating the slow, primitive software that was designed for them 10 or more years ago.

Saddest of the lot is Ontario's ICON I, a revolutionary

computer for its time that was part of an industrial strategy which was supposed to trigger a high-tech revolution. Manufacturers, subsidized by government contracts, bragged of the jobs it would create as the world bought millions of ICONs and then used Ontario-designed software to run them.

Unfortunately, while IBM and Apple jumped ahead a technical generation every few years, doubling their machines' power each time, the ICON lagged behind from the start — even the manufacturing jobs left the country for cheaper labour markets soon after its launch. In the early glory days, the teachers and programmers who developed the new software delivered material designed to match the needs of Canadian schools. Within a few years, however, it became obvious that the tens of thousands of first-generation ICONs that dotted Ontario classrooms were incapable of running the leading-edge programs being designed by the major software corporations. As schools gradually switched to Apple Macintosh and IBM technology, the software fell into disuse, and American-made programs designed for the newer machines usurped the ICON dream.

Today, after placing about 180,000 computers of all makes in its schools, the Ontario government estimates that 25 percent of those computers (those with primitive 8-bit technology) are obsolete. More critical assessments would raise that number substantially by including any computer that is more than seven years old. The problem of outdated equipment is not limited to Ontario, as school jurisdictions across North America find themselves in similar positions. The schools that jumped onto the computer bandwagon first are usually the ones with the oldest equipment. In British Columbia, provincial funding in the mid-eighties paid for Apple Macintosh computers that were revolutionarily easy to use (users could perform many tasks by utilizing an innovative pointing device called a mouse instead of the keyboard). As a result, many teachers were able to incorporate computers into their regular curriculum with fewer problems, and these teachers today are probably significantly ahead of other teachers in terms of computer use.

Unfortunately, though, the small-screened black-and-white monitors and the limited computing power of the early Macs (as they are commonly known) have set limits on their in-class effectiveness. Teachers and students are ready for the high-speed colour machines of the nineties and have developed the skills and the curriculum to use them effectively, but school officials say they cannot afford to buy a new generation of computers. Elsewhere, schools which have lagged behind and are just now buying computers are discovering that the machines cost half their original price and offer 10 times the power. Although they may have delayed a commitment to technology for all the wrong reasons, their tardiness has paid off — at least from a technical standpoint.

What Computer Equipment Belongs in a Classroom?
While many people are tempted to retreat from the nomenclature of the computer world, it is important to learn a few of the basics. This is not as painful a lesson as many fear.

The common parts of a computer work station consist of the computer itself, known as the *central processing unit* (CPU), where all the computations occur; a monitor, which is the screen that displays the computer's efforts; the keyboard, through which commands are typed and sent to the CPU; and a mouse (or, on some models, a roller ball), which is used as a pointing device and can send simple signals to the CPU.

Computers also require *hard drives* for their long-term memory — storage of the information that allows them to run. Often, these hard drives are internal, tucked away in the same plastic box as the CPU, although additional drives can be hooked up externally. When someone writes an essay or draws a picture using the computer, it can be stored on the hard drive and retrieved later. Hard drives usually are connected to a floppy disk drive as well so that new data (programs and files) can be transferred in and out of the machine. Thus a student who works on a computer at home can copy homework from the hard drive onto a floppy disk, carry it to school and, if the two machines speak the same language, add it to the school computer.

Hard drives come in different sizes, and the larger the size (measured in megabytes), the greater the capacity. The earliest personal computers did not have hard drives at all and could handle only the small amounts of information that fit onto a one-megabyte floppy disk. The first hard drives had capacities of 10, 20 or 40 megabytes, but current models tend to be between 100 and 500. Serious users will have 1,000-to-3,000-megabyte drives (called 1 to 3 gigabytes).

Computers also need short-term memory called *RAM* (random access memory) that runs whenever the machine is on. When a student needs to use a game or a story stored on the hard drive, he or she opens its contents onto the RAM portion of the computer so that it can become active. While the intricacies of RAM may seem to be confusing, the capacity or size of the RAM becomes important when assessing what tasks a computer can perform. If there is too little RAM, then there will not be enough capacity to operate complicated (i.e., larger) programs. One of the priorities during the up-grading of old equipment is usually to add extra RAM so that a computer can keep up with the demands of new software.

It becomes clearer if you think of the computer as an office. The screen is the desktop, where you do your work, while the hard drive is the cabinet on the other side of the room, where your calculator (i.e., a spreadsheet program) and files (i.e., a particular letter or assignment) are stored. The RAM is the cart that you use to transfer these things back and forth between where they are stored and where they are used. Having more RAM is the same as having a larger cart on which to move material to your desk so that you can take on more work.

Printers are sometimes found in individual classrooms, although more often a printer is shared by several class-rooms, connected to their computers by cables that snake through the school walls and ceilings. A student can issue a print command from his or her classroom machine and then slip off to the printer's location to pick up the printed material, the so-called hard copy.

There are three main kinds of printers. The older dot-matrix units have a striker pin that hits a typewriter ribbon to create thousands of dots that form images on a page. They were the earliest kind of printer and, because of their notice-able dot patterns, tended to give computer printouts a bad name — solid typewriter script was much easier on the eyes.

Ink-jet printers, more recent additions to schools, use tiny ink sprayers to create dot patterns, but the dots fill in as the ink runs slightly. The better units on the market now can provide very good quality printing of text at a very low price.

Laser printers are based on photocopier technology, using an electrostatically charged drum to trap dry ink on paper. They usually offer exceptionally good quality and, as a result, are the most expensive. But prices have dropped dra-matically in recent years, and quality has continued to go up.

There are different kinds of colour printing available with each kind of printer, from the single-colour ribbons of the dot-matrix printer to the multiple ink reservoirs that allow simple colour reproduction on ink-jet printers. Colour laser printers and various other technologies also exist, but they are aimed at the graphics industry, and any school that boasts a $4,000 colour printer invites scrutiny of its priorities.

Modems are the small electronic boxes that allow the transmission of computer signals across phone lines so that two or more distant computers can talk to one another. They are the link to the information highway that everyone is talking about and are used to transfer information be-tween computers. They may also have a fax component (fax-modem) that allows information to be sent from a com-puter to an ordinary fax printer. Modems convert a comput-er's digital information into a noise that can travel over tele-phone lines and then be decoded by a second modem on the receiving end. (They MOdulate and DEModulate.) Any-one who has accidentally phoned a fax number has heard the kind of signal that modems create.

Software is the digital information that is used by the computer (known as hardware) to perform all its tasks. Without software, a computer is like a television that is not receiving channels or a VCR without a tape — you can plug them in and turn them on, but you won't be able to see or do anything. Thus the purchase of a computer is only a first step, and new users should remember to set aside money to purchase useful software after they have acquired their hardware. Normally, software is bought on one or more floppy disks and transferred onto a computer's hard drive to make it readily available at all times without the hassle of fumbling through a drawerful of disks looking for the right one. Likewise, information can be copied from a hard drive onto a floppy disk and then passed on to another computer.

Software is also being loaded onto *CD-ROM*s (compact disk/read only memory), a new transfer medium that looks identical to audio CDs and is the basis of the new multi-media technology. CD-ROM machines connect to comput-ers the same way that hard drives do, but they only allow the computer to read the contents of a CD-ROM and, unlike a hard drive, cannot have new material added to them. In this, they are similar to record albums and audio CDs, media which allow you to play their contents in whatever order you choose and even copy them but which do not allow changes to be made. The popularity of CD-ROMs is attributed to their low cost of production (although the few cents it costs to press them is not reflected in their retail prices yet) and the fact that they can store 650 megabytes of data, about two to six times the capacity of a typical hard drive. This means that they can hold about 100,000 pages of straight text or, more commonly, be loaded with all the memory-intensive elements of a multimedia information package — voices, animation, pictures, text and music.

We Didn't Have Computers When I Was a Kid. Why Now?
On the surface, there seems to be some merit to the observation that classrooms were computerless for years, and the kids who went on to use them later in life learned about them in college or on the job. After all, the engineers and programmers who design today's new technology probably did not know anything about computers when they were in elementary school during the sixties and seventies. So, we should not be too surprised to hear similar arguments from parents who do not use computers at all and manage to live normal and productive lives without them.

Any adult, whether teacher or parent, who accepts that computers belong in schools without having personally used the technology is making a gigantic leap of faith, a leap that is all the more nerve-racking because of the newness and volatility of the computer-education business. It is far easier to perceive the usefulness of computers in a classroom if a person has already found uses for them in his or her own life. Unfortunately, the technology is only beginning to be used effectively in schools, and there is a limited amount of convincing proof that computers have improved the quality of education to date. Using computers in school in the nineties is like being part of a second wave of settlers to arrive in a new land — there was a lot of work done before your arrival, but there is even more to be done if you are to be successful.

In order to forge ahead and decide to increase the presence of computers in the classroom, then, one has to make a few assumptions.

1. Computers are playing an increasing role in all our lives and are not a passing fad.

2. Computers, with their multiple uses, can become valuable learning tools in a school.

3. Computer use is becoming so pervasive in everyday life, it is important that everyone develops basic computer skills.

4. The earlier a child is introduced to computers, the more comfortable he or she will be around them.

These assumptions are not difficult to make after some careful thought and some basic research. But it is also important to make sure that school officials are working under the same premise and that they are providing their schools with appropriate equipment and fitting it into a solid curriculum.

Why Rush Into It Now? Why Not Wait 10 Years?
Unfortunately, it is probably too late to put off the decision any further. The capabilities of computers have advanced so quickly in the past few years that there is no technical reason to delay their introduction to the classroom. Big advances in speed, dependability and ease of use have already been made, and most of the refinements still to

come will be improvements rather than radical new directions. We do not need to wait for virtual-reality technology capable of simulating space travel or scientific exploration to put classroom computers to good use now.

While the potential of computers in schools is growing daily, it makes sense to integrate them into the classroom now so that teachers and students can progress along with the technology rather than playing catch-up years from now.

Why Not Just Use Computers at Home?

Not surprisingly, that is exactly what is happening already. More than one-third of all Canadian families have at least one computer (compared with 99.3 percent with phones, 62.8 percent with cable TV, 94.9 percent with colour televisions and 78 percent with kitchen stoves or ranges), but the presence of a computer in a home is still very much a function of the parents' income, age, profession and geographical location. According to a 1994 survey by Compas, a market-research company, 66 percent of families with incomes of more than $70,000 had a computer, compared with 21 percent earning less than $30,000; parents with university educations were 2.3 times likelier to have a computer than those with only a high school education. Thus while some children already have home access to word processing, graphics and online services, over half do not even have the use of the simplest computers. Some observers fear that this will cause serious inequities across society by placing information and computing power in the hands of a new class of well-educated, technically competent people. While most people can watch television and even play video games, far fewer have the means to take a more active role in the part of the electronic world that allows users to manipulate, control and create their own information. Already, it is the people with the most money and the best jobs and education who are flocking to learn the intricacies of the new technology.

Will Computers Lead to Employment?

Growing up around computers is unlikely to hurt anyone's chances of getting a job of some sort, but it hardly guarantees a good career launch after high school. Although there is a wide range of philosophies of computer education in school boards across North America, it seems safe to conclude that the trend is shifting toward viewing the computer as a learning tool rather than a subject of specialized study intended to produce job skills. In public schools, at least, more and more people feel that the computer should be used to assist the teaching of math and history rather than being isolated as a subject by itself.

(This commonsense approach, however, may be a long way from reality. The International Association for the Evaluation of Educational Achievement (IEA) 1992 Computers in Education Study found that kids who used computers in schools around the world spent more of their computer time learning about computers than digitally studying all other subjects combined. This was true even in the United States, where, theoretically at least, the emphasis is supposed to be on using the machines as tools rather than treating them as subject matter. In grade 5, fully 50 percent of American students' computer time was spent studying computers. That percentage climbed to 67 percent in grade 8 and 83 percent by grade 11.)

A few years ago, it was common to hear educators debating the merits of software programs or types of hardware in terms of whether students would find them in their future workplace, and amazingly, there are still some public school teachers today recommending complicated computer systems for grade three students because they will provide rudimentary job skills. Fortunately, most of those people are finally starting to realize that in an era of rapid and endless change, they are engaged in a ridiculous discussion. After all, in the 10 years it will take an 8-year-old to prepare for university or a first job, the computer industry will have advanced by five or more new generations. Each generation will double the power and the speed of a computer, which in turn will drive software companies to continue redesigning their programs to take fuller advantage of the improvements. Nothing will remain the same for long — until the advances in technology finally reach their limits.

And even if the pace of change did make it possible to train students for tomorrow's jobs, new computers and software should be chosen on their merits as classroom workhorses, not on the basis of their future relevance in an office or factory.

Aren't Schools Supposed to Train the Workers of Tomorrow?
That depends on who you listen to. Business leaders often talk about getting schools to provide them with graduates

who will meet the needs of employers, but few of those same business leaders are willing to offer job guarantees to students who take their advice and shape their school days around a potential job. Again, change is occurring so rapidly in the workplace that few businesses can even tell what kind of employees they will need in 10 years, so it does not make sense to try to steer education strictly along a business route.

Besides, it is not a good idea to aim a generation of students toward a limited number of careers (computer or otherwise) simply on the notion that certain jobs seem to be in

"With this sort of hand-eye coordination, I'll be ready for a job in space command by next year."

demand now. Eventually, the rush of trained graduates would saturate that job market, leaving a lot of newly graduated specialists unemployed and unable to move easily into other fields. No doubt, the glut of workers would also pull down the wages of what had once been highly prized jobs (a side effect that business leaders seldom mention). Shorter-term specialization at the postsecondary level seems much more beneficial to the students and to society as a whole.

Less often heard is the suggestion that business also wants schools to shape the consumers of tomorrow — with a taste for particular products. Schools are already beginning to experience a corporate presence in their halls as soft-drink bottlers and cosmetic producers find ways to reach teenage consumers early, in the belief that buying habits are often shaped during childhood. Entertainment conglomerates and the communications industry seem to be showing an increased interest in the student market, knowing that there will be large dividends paid in the future by making this generation comfortable with (and even dependent on) their digital products and services.

While business does have a right to concern itself with the quality of graduates coming out of the public and high school system, its concerns are not altruistic enough to be trusted completely. As a result, current education policy-makers are best advised to emphasize the graduation of well-rounded individuals who are able to adapt to a changing world. General literacy and the ability (and willingness) to learn new skills are becoming the new requirements for success after graduation.

The integration of classroom computers throughout the curriculum can help prepare students for a career of continual change, can make them, as the latest catch phrase has it, "lifelong learners" and can give them the skills to cope both socially and economically in the adult world. By effectively adding computers to the school resources that children use every day, educators will fulfill a three-pronged mandate. Computers will improve the delivery of some (not "all" or even "most," just "some") of the current curriculum. They will help develop general computer-related skills that will give students the confidence to live in a world which is becoming technically sophisticated. And, through their use of common software programs and operating protocols, they will teach some basic skills that will serve as a foundation for more specialized skills later on.

Do Boys Use Computers More Than Girls?

The common perception is that nerdy boys hog the computers during the day (then come back for more after school) and that girls never have a chance. And it's true that a quick examination of our cultural stereotypes doesn't turn up a female equivalent of the boy with the too short pants, the plastic pocket protector and the thick glasses, who can answer every math question and fix the school computer system any time it burps. Girls, it has been assumed, do not much interest themselves with computers. Yet that stereotype has been changing as the in-school computer has become less and less a novelty and has been moved from the cloakrooms and closets into the curriculum. The nerdiness associated with computers has mostly disappeared now that all students are expected to become proficient.

The International Association for the Evaluation of Educational Achievement (IEA) 1992 Computers in Education Study found that on a standard test, the mean score for American girls was almost identical to that for boys. It was good news and attracted a lot of media attention at the time of the study's release.

However, the procedures used by the IEA study tested only general familiarity with computers and did not highlight the differences in the way students use them. After the study was released, project director Ronald Anderson of the University of Minnesota emphasized that while the average amount of computer activity in a school might be the same for boys and girls, the pocket-protector brigade was still around — especially in the higher grades. Studies show that advanced Pascal programming classes are filled with many more boys than girls and that more female students in the United States seek proficiency in computer-oriented business skills than other computer-related specialties. No doubt, this will eventually affect their career expectations, as programming and other technical jobs are much higher-paid and better-regarded than positions that require office skills such as word processing and data entry.

In Austria and the Netherlands, where greater emphasis is placed on learning *about* computers instead of how to use them for general purposes, the gender gap is much wider than in America. The theory and science of computers still seems to draw more interest from boys than girls, leaving female students in these countries far behind their male peers. This is worth keeping in mind for parents concerned about gender equity, because a school's approach to computer education can tacitly ease girls away from both the machines and their advantages. If computer use is not smoothly integrated into the regular curriculum but concentrates on programming and configuring hardware, then there is a hidden gender bias at work.

These are important issues to keep in mind if local authorities conduct tests to identify the problems of gender bias. If the raw data says that on average, girls and boys use computers for equal amounts of time, it's important to ask for specifics about exactly how the computers are being used.

Finally, in a March/April 1994 newsletter, the Federation of Women Teachers' Associations of Ontario (FWTAO) laid out the following blistering list of statistics about computer use outside schools. It leaves no doubt that action will have to be taken if the matter of gender bias is to be properly addressed. "Outside of class, 7 percent of teenage girls use computers compared to over 40 percent of the teenage boys. Parents tend to purchase home computers for sons rather than daughters (four to one ratio) and encourage boys to use the home computer more than the girls. There are three times as many boys as girls in summer computer camps. In 1990, girls accounted for 41 percent of students in grade twelve geometry classes, 24 percent in physics classes and 17 percent in computer-studies classes in Canada. Women make up 10.6 percent of computer-education teachers."

To combat this inequity, the FWTAO recommends:

1. Structured scheduling of computer time so that girls and boys receive equal access and encouragement.

2. More female role models, which may mean incentives for women teachers who assume computer-support jobs.

3. Input from girls about how computers could be located and used in schools.

4. A method of evaluating software titles and subject matter so that they will appeal equally to girls and boys.

5. The portrayal in software of equal numbers of males and females, a balance of the sexes in active and passive roles and language that includes females in its scope.

What Is Edutainment Software? Does It Belong in Schools?
Edutainment is the way the software industry slurs together the words *education* and *entertainment*, suggesting that it has developed games that are educational or, conversely, educational material that is fun. The truth, though, is that lots of edutainment software is neither very educational nor fun.

While the edutainment label itself, catchy and self-explanatory, works wonderfully to explain the concept, it should be a red flag for parents and teachers who see it on software. It is a signal to stop and take a close look to decide whether the product it describes is in fact a piece of instructive software that happens to be fun or a game that happens to have educational merit — or whether it is really just a crude attempt to rescue a boring teaching aid with the addition of a bad video game.

The problem is not unique to the world of computers. For the most part, self-consciously educational games and toys loaded with deadly serious content fail when they arrive in the playroom. And, not surprisingly, the ones that do work either weren't designed with education in mind or were the product of people who knew enough to keep their educational benefits well in the background. Monopoly has given several generations of children an insight into basic math skills, and Lego blocks have fascinated children around the world while transforming them into fledgling engineers, designers and architects. But the real reason these products are effective is that kids are having so much fun, they are unaware of the learning process which accompanies the play. To the players, and even the parents, the manipulation of hundreds of fake dollars or dozens of little coloured blocks is a recreational pastime whose academic lessons slip subtly into the subconscious, disguised as fun.

With the success of shoot-'em-up video games during the eighties, a new generation of educational toy makers emerged, looking to attract adult customers (parents) by offering meaningful content in computer games that would entertain children. But bringing the halves together was not a guaranteed recipe for a successful whole. Children are brutal critics of games, especially video games, and also extremely fashion-conscious. Any game that has been clumsily grafted onto a history lesson is bound to be labelled as lame and banished by the mob.

There was a time in schools when spelling bees were an exciting teaching tool; kids competed to see who could spell the most words. To many of us, these contests were a great way to escape the confines of boring dictation textbooks and Friday-morning tests. But when the recess bell rang, spelling immediately gave way to baseball and soccer.

As kids, we realized that even though a teacher could make schoolwork fun and exciting, recess was our own time, when we made our own kinds of fun. We seldom considered combining the two kinds of amusement, and any teacher who tried to bring the two together was doomed to failure. An edutainment baseball game that required a batter to pause before each pitch to spell "extraordinary" or "delicious" or had base runners reciting multiplication tables before advancing around the diamond would have been mercilessly scorned. The same rules apply to software. Many of these educational packages with games built into them are as appealing to children as a chocolate-covered lima bean.

The first wave of educational games consisted of little more than flashcard programs that rewarded users with bleeps and flashing screens for every correct answer. Mathematical tables and phonetics seemed to attract the most attention, but spelling, reading and geography were also covered. Later versions kept the same premise but tried to add value by using colour graphics, more intricate animation and better sound. Although it would be hard to prove, these programs seem to have been developed by small companies with limited resources that survived because of a lack of competition. Their graphics tended to be amateurish, and their educational content was abysmal. In a time when whole-language approaches to reading and spelling have been proved effective for primary and junior grade students and have become the official policy of so many boards, software programs still feature phonetic exercises from the fifties. Most of them are bad, while some border on harmful because they apply outdated and misunderstood educational theory.

Many of the early CD-ROM packages are even worse, and not just because of wrongheaded educational theory either. Buyers of educational software need to be wary of products which may have been thrown together by publishers who have realized that during this period of change, people will still pay outrageous prices for anything in a CD wrapper. Too often, what the buyer gets for $50 to $100 is a disk loaded with a mishmash of graphics, sounds and text that have no relationship to any discernible theme or lesson.

On the other hand, there are some extremely good educational programs that do manage to earn the admiration of kids without resorting to posing as games. Just as some books will attract readers through good design and clever presentation, some software is able to convey important concepts to children in a stimulating, thoughtful way.

Fortunately, there is a growing amount of this sort of good software available for kids, both as reference material and as computer applications. Microsoft, the world's largest software company, has finally recognized the potential of the children's market and seems bent on dominating it by producing good programs at reasonable prices. Its writing and artistic programs for kids have dramatically raised the standards of juvenile word processing and drawing software, while on the reference side of the business, Microsoft has launched a series of interactive CDs such as Encarta, a multimedia encyclopædia (with an American bias) loaded with maps, illustrations, photographs, sound and even some animated film clips. There are hundreds of other companies also contributing to the software market, and more are joining every month.

"And anyone who doesn't find this exercise entertaining or educational can go and have a chat with the principal."

In fact, the entertainment and personal software industry is being transformed as newcomers are rushing into the business after witnessing the meteoric rise of some of the most successful pioneers. Broderbund, an American company specializing in children's software and games, became an industry leader almost overnight, partly because of its translation of some popular American storybooks (Mercer Mayer's *Grandma and Me*, among them). Unfortunately, not many of the companies have met the high standards of the leaders, and some of the worst still hide behind the edutainment label.

Kid Pix (another wonderful product at the heart of Broderbund's astonishing success) arguably provides the most fun that a 6-year-old can have on a computer. With its array of colour stamps, drawing tools, sound effects, alphabets, animation abilities and exploding erasers, it is a beguiling introduction to the creative side of computing. Yet it is no more an edutainment product than crayons and construction paper are. The software provides a fun medium in which kids can exercise their skills and talents. That's all.

The biggest problem with the whole notion of edutainment products is the twofold assumption that education on its own cannot be interesting and that entertainment cannot be enlightening. Anyone who starts with the belief that education is so boring that it must be rescued by the addition of a video game is dashing the chances of producing something worthwhile before the process even begins. Just as Kid Pix is fun and also instructive, there are straightforward educational products that kids find fascinating. It doesn't have to be a game to capture kids' attention. Simm City, a popular consumer game in which players design cities, is an open-ended lesson in civics and urban geography. Such products do not portray themselves as intentional crossover edutainment resources. What they share is high quality and authenticity rather than a desire to exploit that huge education market by riding a catchy slogan to limited success.

Are Computers a Good Device for Educational Material?

For some people, the worry is not about whether a product provides good entertainment or good education but, rather, about the medium itself. They are concerned that the style of recent software is evolving in too many wrong directions, moved along more by its own technical prowess than by its demonstrated ability to serve higher purposes.

History professor and author Theodore Roszak rails against this tendency in his revised edition of *The Cult of Information*: "So much that comes to us out of the culture of computers...grinds away at the already diminished attention span and power of concentration. The essence, after all, of hypertextual surfing is pushing buttons and jumping around....Dazzling? Indeed it is, in the sense of endlessly distracting. What I have been most aware of in dealing with software like this is...the software, which is the work of technicians eager to showcase their skills. But these skills look suspiciously like the skills that go into the one-cut-per-second soft-drink commercials aimed at youthful viewers, all medium with no message deeper than the reflex association of the product with a hundred flashy images."

It is a harsh criticism that can be applied to some of the most successful educational resources available and brings the whole notion of interactive multimedia into question. Certainly, though, it is only a new version of a debate that has raged since books began to replace wandering minstrels and television began to intrude on books.

Not ready to dismiss computer technology from the classroom completely, though, Roszak concludes his tirade with the observation that only when the technology is out of the hands of technicians will teachers know how beneficial it can be in education. "Simply by being there, by surviving and by having as much contact with inquiring minds as possible, [teachers] can help uphold the value of literacy. Our schools can become one of the places that surround information technology with a greater culture that disciplines its excesses." It is an important reminder. During this time when the nature of the technology is determining so much of what goes on, software and hardware alike should be looked to only as resources within teachers' arsenals and not permitted to determine a new agenda.

What About Video Games?
Video games, of course, come in all kinds of styles, from the perfectly simple to the inutterably complex; from the ridiculous gore of Mortal Kombat, where street fighters maim each other, to the sublime graphics of the haunting Myst, a mystical mystery-game-cum-puzzle. And critics are not by any means unanimous in their criticism. True, much of the content is desperately mindless or even horrifying to parents,

but it is undeniable that some games do teach mental skills, such as Tetris, which links a player's lightning-fast trigger finger to an addictive challenge of spatial perception as he or she manipulates falling shapes into places where they will fit.

In fact, there are those who relish the idea of discovering what makes these two-dimensional images on a screen so appealing. Children who declare themselves uninterested in schoolwork will devote hours to sharpening their wits by uncovering and then memorizing the complex strings of commands required to take the idiot plumbers of Nintendo's Marioland through endless mazes. Even though there are few tangible rewards (indeed, the only reward is not having to start all over again), kids practise until they master it and then share their secrets and lessons with their peers in schoolyards and in class.

And whether we see the intrinsic value of video games or not, it's clear that when children discover that knowledge is something you can share with your friends in the schoolyard — or even trade for lunch money — they are already equipping themselves for the economy of the near future in which information promises to be the most active commodity on the world's exchanges.

Parents are well advised to look at the software their children are using in school to make sure that it is appropriate to the curriculum. If kids are simply playing meaningless games or using second-rate educational programs that have nothing to do with what they should be studying, it may be a sign that teachers and principals have been unable to find a meaningful way to fit the computer into their teaching plans or that the administration which brought the computers into the school did not provide adequate software.

How Accessible Should Computers Be?

One of the biggest problems that teachers face with computers is finding a way to fill their administration's computer-time requirement. In Ontario, where provincial regulations call for students to spend two and a half hours per week using a computer, many teachers have been given no training or direction in using the machines in their lesson plans, and it is not uncommon to find computer time going unused or just left as an optional activity. At worst, computer time is sometimes doled out as a reward for good behaviour. This can certainly warp student attitudes toward technology if they begin to perceive computers as an occasional toy provided to keeners rather than a useful tool for everyone.

It is important that there be sensible conditions placed on the use of school computers. Most teachers would not consider restricting a student's use of library books or an encyclopædia; nor would they offer the use of a Nintendo game during schooltime. Thus, while it is up to the teacher to decide how to make the best use of computer equipment within his or her own curriculum, it is also important to understand what message is being sent to the students about the value of computers.

Regular computer access is obviously also dependent on the number of computers available to students. Although impressive-sounding statistics tend to suggest that there is one computer for every 14 to 16 students in the public school system (14 in Ontario, 16 in the United States), the reality is that a single classroom usually has only one or two machines to be shared by as many as 30 kids. (Accurate computer statistics are almost impossible to obtain, as some school boards are laden down with lots of outdated, dysfunctional equipment, while others may have far fewer but better computers.) In those situations, teachers may opt for using the computer as the focus of an activity centre in the classroom that might offer students the opportunity to type assignments and use software relevant to particular parts of their studies.

Although they are the exception, some schools do offer much higher student-computer ratios, but there is seldom a computer for every student, except in some special (and expensive) laboratory settings. Having two to four students sharing a computer at a time is not uncommon, especially in situations where they are gathering information or using an interactive program that encourages group discussion and decision making.

SCHOOLS AND THE
INFORMATION HIGHWAY

The information highway is simply a recently coined term used to describe a network that carries data around the world. Actually, an information pipeline might have been a better metaphor, as it is easier to envision information as a fluid resource that flows to consumers through pipes rather than along highways. But no doubt the marketing mavens who decide such things realized that an image of blasting down a freeway in a sleek automobile was more appealing than moving water (or ooze) through a pipe, and the highway image stuck. The information highway, then, is nothing more than a symbol of the way we will communicate in the coming years.

There are, of course, a number of more familiar pipelines already in place, and most of us are linked up to at least two of them:

There is the pipeline that cable companies use to direct television programs into our homes. Like a gravity-fed water pipe, its content flows in one direction only and floods into our homes with the flick of a switch. Just think of your TV remote control as a high-tech shut-off valve.

And there is the phone-company pipeline that lets us connect to anyone else who has a telephone or a fax machine. Although it allows for a two-way flow of communication all the way around the world, it often uses a narrower pipe that limits the amount of information which can be moved. The multistrand coaxial cable used to move television signals can carry the broad-band signals that translate into colour pictures and stereo sound, but the traditional narrow-band copper wire of phone companies is best for moving the simpler voice signals of conversations and the digital information which drives fax machines. In recent years, however, phone companies around the world have been switching to fibre optic cable that can carry hundreds of light signals at a time, greatly enhancing its potential loads. With fibre optic cable comes the reality of the picture phones that *Popular Mechanics* magazine was hailing back in the sixties.

For the past 30 years, the cost of communicating with one another over these two pipelines has dropped considerably, and as a result, their use has gone up quite sharply. We get more TV channels all the time, and people use the phones more than ever, but there would be little talk of Information Superhighways if it were not for another system that is not just growing but is doubling in size every year — the Internet.

What Is the Internet?

As early as the late seventies, the American military and its research facilities began to send information back and forth among military computers over secure telephone networks to speed up the process of communication and to provide reliable links around the continent during the Cold War. The system they set up did not look like a regular phone sys-

"Madame Zimba sees that your first trip on the information highway will be short but expensive. Very expensive. Do you want a receipt?"

tem with big trunk lines branching out to hook up single users. Rather, they created a network, a web, so that in the event of attack or sabotage, information could always reroute around a disrupted line. The system worked well enough that scientific agencies such as the National Aeronautics and Space Administration and the National Science Foundation joined in, although they did so for less politically strategic reasons. By 1981, the Internet linked 200 large computers, allowing their users to move freely from one to the other without leaving their chairs.

At first, the traffic came from scientists sharing their latest findings and asking for more information from their colleagues, but it soon became a common practice to use the Internet for less academic pursuits. As more academic institutions came online, staff and students began to correspond with their counterparts around the world without the high cost of regular telephone charges. By 1991, there were a few million Internet users who gained access to the system through any one of 300,000 computer sites in colleges, businesses and government departments. While the amount of academic and scientific material flowing over the lines increased greatly, so did the number of personal electronic messages known as E-mail and informal discussion groups that would come together daily via computer keyboards to "talk" about politics and literature or movies and sports. And sex and anarchy.

Anarchy, of course, is just the topic for Internet conversation, because thanks to the cunning military minds that invented the uninterruptible weblike system, the shape of the Internet and the rate at which it grows cannot be controlled by any one group. No one "runs" the Internet. No one decides how it will be used.

By late 1994, no one could even accurately guess the number of people roaming the Internet, but approximately 3.2 million institutions had made their computers available as entry points to it. While early Internet users had to be located near the huge computers that made up the network, the advent of personal computers with modems made access much easier, allowing anyone with a phone line and the correct password to contact a host computer from home or the office and enter the net. As many as 50 million users in 1994 explored the Internet regularly, some on serious business, others, spurred by curiosity, merely poking around the archives and libraries of information that the member institutions make available. While the common term for such perusal is "surfing," a more appropriate comparison for new users is to the dark and confusing world of caves and the sport of spelunking. Because it was not born of a master plan or common standards, the Internet is a confusing place to navigate, and only the most adroit user can find his or her way around its labyrinth of information with ease.

Is the Internet the Information Highway?
Fascination with the Internet and the potential to travel digitally around the world has spawned all the hype for an Information Superhighway, but in truth, the Internet is more a world of typed characters and numbers than anything else. While graphics, cartoons and pictures, even lim-

ited animated sequences, are becoming available, the treasures to be gleaned are not as rich as many newcomers expect. In theory, it is similar to being given access to the best libraries of the world, but in fact, it is more akin to being dumped in a vast uncharted subway network with no map and only a faint hope of finding one's way to the most interesting graffiti — and even less hope of finding a real book. Not only do you have to locate, for example, a university campus along one of the unmarked train lines without getting lost or mugged, you then have to pick your way to its library and search endless bookshelves until you find the volume you want. There are few signs and even fewer actual human assistants to ease the journey. Yet somehow, the Internet generates such enthusiasm that for millions of people, the thrill of the search remains as valuable as reaching the destination. Sometimes the intrepid explorer stumbles across interesting gems of information or meets fellow Internet travellers in unexpected places. More often, perhaps — for newcomers at least — the journeys become a challenging game of navigation that ends in failure. At least these spelunkers can simply return to base camp by disconnecting, then start over again by dialling back into the host computer. It can be an exciting pastime for a generation that grew up playing Dungeons and Dragons.

One should not get too discouraged about the current limits of these networks, though, for the information highway is still under construction. No doubt, the pioneers who settled Canada were equally split over the value of the superhighways of their day. To the voyageurs who made their living traversing the rapids of the Ottawa River en route to Montreal from the West, the rivers and lakes of the wilderness must have seemed a wonderful access route to the wealth of the frontier. Years before canals, highways and railroads were built, visionaries talked of improved communication and links with the whole world, while skeptics must have poked their toes in muddied oxcart tracks and wondered when such dreams would be realized. It took engineers, entrepreneurs and politicians centuries to design a transportation system that was more suited to general commerce and the conveyance of ordinary passengers. And that is what is happening on the Internet now.

When Will the New Information Highway Be Complete?

The information highway is very much a work-in-progress, but not one based on clear plans, compatible standards and careful budgeting. Just as railroad companies raced around the globe in the 19th and early 20th centuries trying to outmanoeuvre their competitors, cable TV companies are today arguing with telephone companies over the rights to carry information into homes, businesses — and schools. Predictably, most of the debate is being waged by American corporations that tend to neglect the rest of the world in their plans, and while newcomers like Viacom talk of pumping commercial services directly into homes, longtime Internet users represented by American organizations such as the Electronic Frontier Foundation are making forceful arguments against allowing new services to be patterned after the old profit-driven model of one-direction cable-television feeds. Users, they maintain, should be able to send out more than pizza orders and movie requests along the network. If the Internet continues to operate as a multi-directional web, anyone will be able to offer information or entertainment in a form that anyone else will be able to access. Watchdog organizations also worry that their low-cost access to the worldwide web is about to become very expensive, as big business shapes the next generation of the highway, and that the very nature of the Internet will change and its potential will be compromised if commercial priorities are given sway.

Where Does the Information Highway Actually Go?
It is important that all the candy-coated predictions about the Information Superhighway be kept entirely clear of decisions about Internet access in today's schools.

While the Internet, with its millions of users and its international scale, seems to fire the enthusiasm of many of our current media enthusiasts, when they actually start talking about the coming information highway, they are talking about something else. They ignore the Internet's clumsy interface, poor mapping and limited treasures. Instead, they talk of 500 television channels, in-home shopping, instant delivery of digital video games, movies and music, video conferencing and millisecond electronic mail service. They describe a world of colour pictures, high-fidelity sound and instant gratification — a world where residents need never leave their homes to be part of the world community.

While promoters of the companies that want to hook us

into the information highway fumble for grander descriptions of the new lifestyles their customers will enjoy (and remember, we are really just paying customers in their minds), the truth is that few of those companies can tell just what will flow through the cables which they want to bring to us. Given the national outrage that tore through the country in late 1994 when several Canadian cable companies tried to charge their customers an extra $36 a year for eight new cable channels, 500 TV channels may be of little interest. People may still enjoy physically visiting libraries and video stores in search of entertainment but want devices that let them turn home appliances on and off by phone or video conferencing facilities that allow them to meet teachers during the school day without having to leave work.

No doubt, the highway users of tomorrow will be neither as intellectual nor as slovenly as some companies predict, and many entrepreneurs will go broke trying to sell us their particular vision — just as railroad hucksters whose tracks went nowhere and were of the wrong gauge disappeared in the face of more useful transport services.

Already a number of commercial online services have sprung up offering limited ties to the Internet while also selling access to their own data bases. Statistics indicate that by early 1995, about 5 percent of Americans subscribed to such American-based companies as CompuServe, GEnie and America Online, whose users dial into these networks and explore their offerings. America Online is a relative newcomer to the business but had attracted 1.5 million users by January 1995 — a time when it estimated that it was handling one million connections a day. For about $10 (U.S.) a month, customers get five hours on the system before hourly rates kick in, and they have the run of such traditional information carriers as newspaper and magazine stories from dozens of publications (including *The New York Times, Time* magazine, *Consumer Reports, Road and Track* and *Atlantic Monthly*) as well as access to specialized services and data bases from hundreds of computer companies, special-interest groups and ad hoc discussion groups. There are want ads for everything from automobiles, computers and real estate to marriage partners; movie reviews; shopping services; even nightly live phone-in forums where noteworthy guests type responses to questions and comments from the subscribers.

These services tend to be expensive to use on a regular basis, but they also have proved that people are willing to pay for access to information. Much of that money has been invested in designing easy-to-use interfaces for noncomputer types, and data banks have been loaded with some useful and interesting material which is relatively easy to find. Their biggest appeal lately, though, is that such services are starting to offer entry onto the Internet. Members can send E-mail messages to anyone else who has links to this electronic world, and every subscriber has a mailbox that can be reached by any of the 50 million Internet users. A two-page letter can travel across North America in a matter of seconds, even with computerized files attached to it, allowing people to share digitized manuscripts, photographs or software programs. There are no stamps and no waiting involved.

Should Kids Be Allowed to Play on This Highway?

Commercial interests, almost deranged in their desperate hurry to find a place alongside the Information Super-highway, have utterly confused the issue of how new electronic media can or cannot serve schools.

All the media hype and sex appeal — along with a good dose of Canadian government subsidies — have resulted in a massive networking of classrooms and little else. Common sense has not played a big role in the move to link schools to the Internet, which for now is the only vaguely educational part of the information highway we have available.

The corporate and government visionaries who are in charge of firing up the public's imagination and enthusiasm have put schools high on their agendas, of course. As government agencies publish reports about linking schools with the rest of the world to maintain world-class standards, phone and cable companies have urged schools to bring lines into the classroom so that students will not be left behind.

Suddenly, school officials who cannot even program the time of day on their living room VCRs and have resisted upgrading the pathetic computers that sit idle in their classrooms have become advocates of the information age. With government subsidies, they are going to attach phone lines to schools to give students access to the rest of the world, whether it makes sense or not.

Yet simple prudence dictates that they take time out to explore the technology which they are about to inflict on their teachers and students.

What Equipment Is Needed to Join the Net?

Though some schools do have the expertise to make trips along the Internet worthwhile, they are a very small minority. While most of the others have old computers capable of puttering along the net, they have inexperienced staff and are cursed with older buildings, which in many cases will have to be rewired just so that all classrooms will have

"Gee, Dad, it worked great at first, but there seems to be some interference on the network now."

reliable access to the outside phone line.

Once the phone line is brought into the school, it will have to be hooked up to a modem (price: $100 for an old, slow model to $500 for a fast one that can also send faxes), which will in turn be hooked up to a computer (known as a server) that will act as a hub within the building, transmitting incoming and outgoing signals to and from each computer on the school's network. The phone line will be an ordinary line, perhaps subsidized by a phone company or the government, that will link the school to an Internet gateway. Most universities in Canada have at least a pilot program with a few local schools allowing limited use of their Internet connection, but for schools outside major cities, where such gateways are usually located, long-distance connections will have to be made. Some boards already have Internet access for their mainframe computers, and in Ontario, there are initiatives under way to connect school boards to government networks and Internet access. The use of toll-free 800 phone lines is also possible, but they are not really free, as the sponsor of the number must pay for the calls.

Traditionally, phones in schools have been the domain of secretaries and principals, and an examination of how they are used in your community schools may provide some insight into how prepared a school is for the information highway. If your school has only one phone line that is not easily accessible to staff and there is no fax machine in the office or voice mail, it may be time to suggest that officials improve community access to its staff before plunging into international communications. After all, if voice mail — an invention that allows for inexpensive, low-tech but instantaneous communication 24 hours a day directly to teachers — has not found its way into a school, why the sudden interest in instant communication? Many school boards still rely on their own inefficient in-house courier services to deliver memos to teachers by truck instead of simply sending faxes or E-mail over existing phone lines. In large rural boards, vans travel thousands of kilometres a week moving mail that is old news by the time it finally arrives at distant schools. For many schools, the emphasis should be on local improvement rather than national or international connectivity.

On the other hand, if the school already has the basics of everyday business communication, then maybe a venture into the world of electronic mail, bulletin boards and even the Internet makes sense.

What Can Students Do Once They Get on the Internet?
Access to the Internet has two main uses. Users can tap into information from a fantastically wide variety of sources, mainly as text, without pictures or graphics, and they can communicate with other users. In both cases, the information they find and the "conversations" they have can be copied instantaneously and brought into (downloaded to) the user's computer for later reading.

Communicating over a computer is similar to letter writing or even memo writing, but there is more to it than that. Live sessions can consist of two (or even several) people typing messages to one another in a written simulation of a seminar or a cocktail party. Sometimes the interaction resembles a forum, with a featured guest who can be interrupted with questions from the audience. More commonly, users post comments on computer bulletin boards, responding to messages left by other users. Everything is open to public view, and any of the correspondents may invoke the wrath or adoration of hundreds of other bulletin-board readers with a simple note. Most people on the Internet also have personal mailboxes where electronic mail can be sent. People who have met over bulletin boards will often swap E-mail addresses so that further conversations can be held privately.

What Do Educators Want?
The communication element seems to have the broadest appeal to school officials who are bringing classrooms full of participants online. Using moderators from universities, government agencies or museums, dozens or even hundreds of classrooms can participate in experiments, surveys and interactive projects. In the United States, for example, the National Geographic Society runs a kids' network for grades four to six in conjunction with the National Science Foundation. Using computers, classes of 30 student-scientists investigate such subjects as acid rain, solar energy, food and trash, working with their own teachers (who have in-class resources) and with students from other classes around the world (including Canada) under the direction of National Geographic moderators.

This approach seems to be the most popular, and a number of museums and other educational organizations offer similar programs. Teachers prepare themselves and their classes before the telecommunication part of the course begins and spend time during the few weeks of the course supervising experiments and research by the students. Data and observations are posted on electronic bulletin boards so that anyone else within the program can watch the results unfold. Students in British Columbia and Ontario conducting tests on their local lakes in search of clues to the effects of acid rain will find themselves part of a group that may represent dozens of other provinces and states. By the end of the six-week program, the participants will have a broader view of whatever subject they studied than if their exploration were restricted to their own neighbourhood. They will also realize that their community is part of a much larger society living on a small interconnected planet.

Educationally, these seem to be sound principles, but it is also important to realize that the classroom teacher is an integral part of the program. While the computer and the long-distance connections make any project more appealing to many kids, the value of the lessons learned perhaps could be presented as effectively by a team of teachers using the same published material and working within their own school districts. (Interestingly, about 75 percent of a $600 National Geographic Society course fee pays for such in-class materials as videotapes, textbooks, manuals and student workbooks, while the rest goes toward the cost of 120 minutes of network time — an average of four minutes' telecommunicating per student during the 30-school-day unit.)

Who Is Using the Net Now?

The Consortium for School Networking (CSN), an American organization, is an active proponent of networking for all grades, and it coordinates the efforts of educators who develop ideas for using the Internet to enrich education. Using the bulletin boards that CSN manages on such commercial online services as America Online as well as the Internet itself, members share ideas for network links between students and teachers and also ask questions of their fellow advocates. Unfortunately, the CSN's own bulletin board seems to highlight the problems of online life; it is loaded with more silly questions than good ideas. To

"I'm getting the hang of it now."

the casual peruser, it seems that there is no one around to answer those questions either. Many of the postings come from questioners who could probably handle their own queries with a little research, but the spontaneous nature of bulletin boards makes it really easy to ask anything that pops into your head. This is a problem that afflicts all bulletin boards, not just that of the CSN, and is one of the irritants to anyone who dreams of sharing interesting ideas with his or her peers on the net.

Typical missives on the CSN's board consist of pleas for toll-free access to the Internet or directions on how to find something meaningful to explore once on the net and requests for budget strategies guaranteed to wring computer dollars out of tightfisted school boards or for curriculum guidelines that are relevant to the Internet; and there are also lots of invitations to telecommunicate. Many of the messages exude enthusiastic bewilderment from novices who one day may transform themselves into skilled users. Everything is new, which means that tried-and-true techniques are in short supply.

Obviously, this medium can be a powerful tool for teachers to communicate with one another, to share lesson plans and to extend the walls of the classroom, but so far, it isn't always clear to teachers how to make those things happen.

"I begin teaching a section on creative writing in three weeks," reads one typical note. "We plan to use a book of [author's name deleted] writing prompts....It might be fun to link up with another group of 11th graders doing creative writing at the same time. Gimme a yell."

Clearly, the immediacy of this medium can make net-worked teaching open to spontaneous ideas and approaches that would never survive if teachers had to rely on letters and the mail system to share them. But this particular note went out just three weeks before the teacher's creative-writing unit was scheduled to start. His class might have lucked into a great interaction with several other classrooms of budding authors, but more likely, the network part of the unit failed through lack of preparation. Sometimes the speed of electronic communication seduces people into replacing careful planning with a half-baked idea that would have been best left alone. Online classrooms are still a good idea in theory and will one day be a good idea in practice. For the moment, however, the reality is that a good deal of confusion reigns, and the same professional standards which teachers bring to their classroom activities and preparation are not always found in the electronic realm.

Who Do Students Talk to on the Net?

Student communication is equally revealing. While the National Geographic Society offers some student bulletin boards so that discussions between participants can continue after their formal science units are over, few of the post-project discussions involve science. Requests for pen pals — an honourable and age-old pastime for schoolchildren — seem to be the highest priority of the participants, although the most spirited exchanges come from video-game aficionados, who are happy to post detailed and fairly complicated strategies for winning extra lives in a wide assortment of Nintendo and Sega games. Not surprisingly, even with computers and telecommunication hookups, kids tend to stick to the same topics of conversation. The fact that you're having electronic recess in the global schoolyard doesn't change the things you want to talk about.

What Else Can Kids Do?

The alternate use of Internet hookups — access to information and other resources — is still in a development stage when it comes to the needs of most elementary and secondary students. The online library resources were developed for use by the university and business communities, so even when a secondary school net surfer finds his or her way to a source, the waiting mound of policy briefs, research papers and manuscripts may have limited appeal.

The commercial online services tend to be more useful or at least more interesting, but they are not free. They are, in fact, quite expensive if used regularly. Most of them offer a number of resources for students, working with such large entertainment and publishing companies as Disney and Scholastic to obtain interesting material. Museums, government agencies and educational institutions also contribute to the mound of archived material waiting to be downloaded (copied) to personal computers for leisurely perusal. The National Library in Washington usually has some electronic version of its current displays, giving users a taste of exhibitions that would have normally been available only to Washington visitors. The Smithsonian Institution, like the National Geographic Society, offers a limited number of classroom information kits, but much of the material is related to mail-order packages that must be purchased. Clearly, though, business and educational institutions are trying to find new ways to attract people, and offering educational services electronically is a very popular and cost-effective public-relations gesture.

Is There Any Canadian Content Available to Kids?
The current emphasis in Canada seems to be getting schools tied into the Internet. Working with the provinces,

the federal Department of Communications is setting up SchoolNet, a system that will tie each classroom directly to the outside world. Not surprisingly, Canadian content is lagging way behind the wiring process.

In the context of the rapid change that is sweeping North America, the content lag is understandable and begs for a chicken-and-egg comparison. Do you provide wired links first and have nothing significant to transmit, or do you build an educational infrastructure full of great services but have very few customers who can receive it? The current mood in Canada seems to favour keeping up with the wiring needs on the assumption that content will follow.

The early cable-television industry of the sixties and seventies faced a similar predicament when there were very few Canadian television outlets to carry. Rogers Communications Inc. (one of the country's cable pioneers and now a corporate giant) and the others simply filled their capacity with American content and weathered two decades of accusations that they were doing nothing to promote Canadian channels. Certainly there are serious reasons to draw parallels between the current cable TV networks and the new SchoolNet being built now.

Interestingly, the cable situation did not change significantly until early 1995, with the launch of eight new Canadian cable networks (whose initial programming relied heavily on American and British productions). Even after the long wait for more Canadian offerings, subscribers complained about the cost (roughly $3 extra a month for all eight) and argued loudly that they preferred the established

American channels over the newer Canadian ones. Cultural critics accused the cable companies of poisoning the minds of subscribers against the new Canadian content with unfair pricing policies in the hope that the new networks would die off quickly, while couch potatoes across the country grumbled that the new stations were not as good as their American counterparts. Somehow over the years, the stop-gap measure of filling blank channels with American content had become the status quo, and few people were willing to pay to improve the situation.

Are We Stuck With American Content Forever?
If the SchoolNet scenario unfolds in the same way, there is a possibility that federal and provincial governments will exhaust their resources stringing wire to all the schools and then have nothing left to pay for material to make the network worthwhile as a Canadian cultural resource. If that happens, teachers on the net will be left to improvise by adapting American resources to the needs of their students and scrambling to fashion their own original material and projects in the hope that they will be worth the attention of other users in the same position.

The risks are that after millions of tax dollars have been spent running wire to classrooms, there may be a reluctance to spend more to make the holdings of the national library or the public archives accessible by computer. Museums may not get the funds necessary to teach Canadian history and geography digitally, and art galleries and theatre groups may be unable to find the support needed to create multimedia interfaces for network visits.

That said, then, parents must keep two things in mind:

1. All the excitement generated by the wiring of schools, their connection to the Internet and the establishment of initiatives such as SchoolNet does not mean that the job is done and that useful content has yet been put before children in school.

2. The political will and support that are pushing through these kinds of developments must be maintained if the monies invested already are to pay dividends by bringing Canadian resources into schools.

TEACHERS

When parents are trying to understand why their children are not getting a very good computer education at school, they may be inclined to look at the teachers and ask, "Are these people part of the problem?"

The simplest answer is "yes," and a longer answer is "sort of." But the most relevant answer is "probably yes, but it is not really their fault."

Teachers, of course, get blamed for just about everything that goes wrong in the school system, so it makes sense that they are serving as the fall guys for the computer mess (along with the behaviour mess and the literacy mess and maybe even the budget mess). They are certainly handy targets, much easier to find than school board officials or provincial bureaucrats, so if a child's education falls short in some way, why not blame the teacher? If a child cannot read or write well, the teacher obviously has failed to do his or her job. Maybe if you ignore the issues of overcrowded class-

*"No, Ms. Ryan, the manual says to plug it in
AFTER you remove it from the box."*

rooms and reduced support services, the current trend toward teacher bashing could be rationalized. But, mercifully,
that is a debate which is beyond the scope of this book.

Our concern here is the lack of computer expertise in
the classroom and the inability of teachers to teach children
how to use computers appropriately. Even now, neanderthal
critics (many of whom seem to find their way into school
board politics — and administrations) continue to lay the
blame on the teachers. Their argument goes like this: we

have spent taxpayers' dollars for over a decade, filling the schools with computers, but the teachers have not bothered to learn how to use them. A favourite prehistoric solution to the problem is, of course, to make computer literacy a job requirement and to fire the teachers who don't meet it.

Luckily, cooler heads have prevailed lately, and they are coming to a more sensible conclusion: it is as important to teach the teachers about technology as it is to buy equipment, and it is also imperative to foster interest and enthusiasm for computers in school staffs.

Today, it is easy to ask in retrospect why no one reached this conclusion a long time ago, but it is safe to assume that provincial education ministries did not consult many teachers before they decided to start putting computers into classrooms in the late seventies. Even if teachers had complained that they were not able to shoulder the burden of computer education, their bosses hardly would have repeated those concerns too loudly for fear of losing the provincial grant money which accompanied an interest in computers. This *top-down* implementation of policy is a common theme in any large organization undergoing change, and the teaching profession is especially susceptible to it. Every time the provincial ministry, the local board or the school principal makes a decision about classroom management, it falls on the teachers to implement it, whether they are convinced of its value or not. Since teachers actually control what goes on in the classroom, it only makes sense that they should be at the centre of any process which aims to change classroom activity.

Why Are Teachers Reluctant to Use Computers?

In 1990, the average teacher in the United States was 40 years old and had over a decade of teaching experience. Applying those statistics to Canada, we can assume that most of our teachers are also middle-aged adults who are experienced at what they do and feel that they know what works for them and what does not. They did not experience computers during their own school days and were probably already classroom professionals when educational computing first became an issue. What's more, they have seen their share of failed innovations and less-than-successful experiments (not all of which involved computers) and have been the repeated bottom-end victims of top-down policy strategies. The one thing most of them know about computers is that every new idea which comes along at first attracts enthusiastic supporters who will proclaim it to be the answer to all of public education's ills, real and imagined, before it is abandoned in favour of a new innovation.

As a rule, teachers do not fall into a demographic group that is likely to experiment with computers, and they have had few good reasons to change. Over the past decade and a half, they have seen governments dump machines into schools for appearance' sake without a firm plan for their use. Although teachers have received no compulsory computer training, they have had "computing" added to their job descriptions and have been given vague criteria to fulfill. Even teachers who are interested in computers have discovered that little support is available, and less-than-enthusiastic novices often find that training and equipment are consumed by the teachers who already work with computers. Sometimes, it is plain old-fashioned favouritism at work, but other times, it is a cynical attempt to create a technological showpiece that will give the public an illusion of technological progress. Critics of the Peel County Board of Education, west of Toronto, point to Oakville's River Oaks School as a model school with lots of top-quality equipment and with a heavy emphasis on classroom computing that does not reflect the reality of the rest of the board. While weekly tours of its facilities garner headlines around the world, neighbouring schools are still using the outdated computers commonly found in most other districts. (Its defenders point out that the River Oaks staff simply used its discretionary budget differently than the board's other schools and that major components of its hardware resources came from donations by local high-tech companies. According to its supporters, an enthusiastic staff and creative business partnerships were the driving force behind the school's success.) Only time will tell whether these pilot projects at showplace schools translate into better times for other schools in the system.

Futurists did not help warm teachers' attitudes toward technology when they began predicting that a carefully deployed network of computers in a school could reduce the need for teachers. The earliest of these predictions appeared in popular magazines alongside predictions of flying cars and robotic servants (à la the Jetsons), but their promise of reduced labour costs survived. After all, if computers could replace other skilled workers, why not teachers?

Computers are going to have to get a whole lot faster than anyone is even predicting right now before they can keep up with a roomful of students. Even though teachers were likely the first to understand that computers wouldn't actually be taking over their jobs, their fear that the machines could encourage even larger-sized classes is fairly realistic.

Despite the fact that the talk about computers as "teachers in a box" has pretty well disappeared, there are still a few other disincentives for flesh-and-blood teachers to buy into the computer revolution. While computer advocates are demanding more investment in technology, teacher salaries have been frozen or cut back and classroom sizes have indeed grown. Cutbacks have reduced support services for special-needs children; high school de-streaming and classroom integration have forced teachers to cope with broad differences in the abilities of students in the same class; and workloads have grown correspondingly. At the same time, public education has come under attack by religious traditionalists, political right-wingers, big business, tax reformers, charter schools and education-for-profit corporations.

Little wonder, then, that teachers as a whole haven't rushed to jump onto the computer bandwagon, giving up their weekends to study the mysteries of CDs, servers, networks and Internet news groups.

Yet with all that said, it is not clear whether teachers today are all that reluctant to use computers in their classrooms. For years now, most teachers, like the rest of us, have probably felt pressure to become more computer-literate, and many of them are starting to teach themselves at home or through college extension courses. Good teachers, after all, are constantly on the lookout for ways to keep student interest high. With the elementary school's emphasis on multiple activity centres spread around the classroom, teachers are finding that computers can offer children a stimulating change of venue in learning.

Parents who want to increase the level of computer use in their children's schools but worry that they might uncover reluctance on the part of teachers might be in for a surprise. Chances are good that a parent interested in change may find an eager ally in a teacher who knows where the holdups are and where the need is greatest and who has heard all the administration's excuses a thousand times before.

Will Computers Make Teachers Better at Their Jobs?

A good teacher can become even better with decent tools — be they books, chalkboards or computers. But computers cannot transform bad teachers into good teachers.

By the same token, possessing computer skills does not mean that young teachers fresh out of university are necessarily better than their more experienced counterparts. Knowing how a specific data base program works, for instance, will not help a young teacher deal with a 6-year-old who continually spits into the keyboard or an unhappy adolescent who cannot concentrate on the work. What is important is the ability to mix computer-based resources with other material to make them part of a meaningful instructional activity. Consequently, boards cannot simply wait, as some people suggest, until a process of attrition replaces all those pre-computer veterans. (Besides, the consensus seems to be that few teachers' colleges are turning out computer-literate graduates anyway.)

The knowledge and practical experience of teachers who are already in the classroom must influence the agenda for establishing and implementing computer policy. Too many mistakes have already been made following the lead of technical, administrative and political decisions, and it is time to empower teachers to pursue a more practical approach. Give teachers what they need, and help them incorporate technology into their classes.

What Can Teachers Do With Computers?

As far as teachers are concerned, computers can provide help in three broad categories:

1. Recordkeeping and administrative duties.
2. Instruction and classroom activity.
3. Online communication.

When applied to administrative tasks, computers can win allies easily, and teachers should be no exception. Already, many school boards require teachers to fill out student report cards by computer, and when the system is set up properly, offering both flexibility and term-to-term continuity, the electronic report card is a godsend. Because computers can be tied into administrative records and months' worth of test scores and assignment grades, teachers can speed up their assessments and shorten the tedious work of tabulating and compiling hundreds of pieces of information.

As well, computers also have a role in the other kinds of

records teachers must keep: attendance, student records and milk/lunch/pizza/class-trip money. Letters home to parents of younger students are easier to produce with a good word processing program than with a typewriter; lesson plans and handouts can be produced faster and then kept on file for next year (and are easily modified to suit a new class). The computer does not change the nature of what the teacher does, it simply makes the work less time-consuming and better organized.

If properly managed, computerized records can even be of use to students. While traditional schooling seems to dictate that students seldom see their records, many teachers are discovering that making selective information about assignments and marks available to students can help encourage better work habits. Class lists of grades and the results of assignments and tests could be too embarrassing to post on bulletin boards, but making such information privately accessible to individual students through files protected by passwords would allow them to judge their progress throughout the year without having to wait for term report cards.

In terms of classroom instruction, teachers who use computers as a classroom aid today are pioneers in a promising and fast-growing field. Once they have mastered a few basic software programs common to most school boards, they can begin to create their own teaching materials — as teachers have been doing since the days of the hand-cranked Gestetner copying machine. Of course, computers are quite a bit cleaner and faster than the messy old Gestetners and make it easier to customize material in half a dozen different ways to suit the needs of particular kids in a class. Teachers can include extra work for the advanced learners and simpler material for the slower ones. Having the material in digital form on easily transferable disks also allows teachers to exchange resources and lesson plans with one another and reduces the clutter of desks and briefcases.

As teachers become more familiar with computers, they can get more ambitious, even adapting (or creating) software for use on the students' machines. If a class wants to produce a newspaper, there are word processing and desktop publishing programs that generate impressive-looking finished work, and kids — just like adults — get excited about the way a computer can give their written work the finished look and authority of a published document.

Spreadsheet programs, like word processing software, were not originally designed for the classroom, but a group of students with a pile of raw data and a basic spreadsheet can do everything from weather predictions to complex demographics. Given a body of information to play with and a program capable of sorting it, kids can form hypotheses and then test them, learning the basics of scientific research.

Even the collection of milk money can become an educational resource. If the orders and payments are entered every day on a data base instead of on a scrap of paper, students can do a statistical analysis of their own activity: discovering who drinks what and when and keeping a running tally of how much is spent as the year progresses. Since spreadsheets are all about basic arithmetic and relationships between numbers, the programs are useful from the earliest grades.

Should Teachers Use the Internet?

The idea of linking teachers to one another and to the rest of the world by computer is probably a good one. As they establish stronger links to professional resources, teachers will gain extra tools for searching out ideas and information for their students, which is a boon at a time when cutbacks mean that more traditional resources such as books and specialty magazines are being chopped from budgets.

A major problem in the computerization of the school system has been a lack of training for the teachers. While they are supposed to accommodate and inspire their students' use of technology, teachers have had little personal experience with it themselves. By surfing the Internet in their spare time, they deepen their own interest as they acquire new skills — and can even meet their peers across the country to exchange ideas and information.

In 1993, the Ontario Teachers' Federation (OTF), tired of government inaction, launched its own communications network, designed exclusively for the use of its 130,000 members. Dubbed The Electronic Village, it was supposed to serve as an electronic meeting place for Ontario educators so that they could exchange ideas with one another as well as have access to library catalogues and published documents. The founders expected a few hundred users within the first year and were stunned when 6,000 rushed to sign up within months. Ten percent turned into regular users who could be found on the service late at night and sometimes at dawn.

Even the Ministry of Education took note of the fervour that OTF members displayed for this very practical introduction to computer communications. By early 1994, the Ministry had announced that it would take over the Village, expanding it to several telephone hubs across the province to make access easier and cheaper and encouraging all 128 Ontario school boards to take advantage of its benefits. The government, it seemed, had realized that giving teachers the tools to explore their own corner of the Internet would speed up their acceptance of technology and give the Ministry a powerful communications tool which could cover the huge province efficiently. In fact, 85 percent of the first wave of new Village members were from outside Toronto, a statistic which was often quoted to reinforce the feeling that teachers wanted better links with the provincial education community. But there is still some debate as to when the Village will fulfill that need effectively.

After a few preliminary visits to the early model of The Electronic Village, one can safely assume that many first-time users never return for a second look. While the interface that the teachers use to communicate with the Village is somewhat friendlier than the standard Internet experience, it is not particularly good and discourages all but the most determined visitor. It is filled with idiosyncrasies that make it difficult to understand and forces teachers to learn awkward computer protocols which many of the commercial online services have abandoned.

Still, for those with the patience to learn to make their way from conference to conference, The Electronic Village provides a forum for dozens of specialized interests and allows teachers to share ideas about teaching methods and to trade lesson plans. Even students' work may find its way online as teachers share their ups and downs with one another. Any parent who has wondered what teachers talk about after work would be alternately amused and heartened to peruse the messages that members leave on bulletin boards for one another.

One exchange took place between teachers discussing a story about high school students using their own local electronic bulletin boards to swap essays with one another, boosting marks through plagiarism. Rumour had it, explained a teacher, that for $20, young information bandits could buy a computer disk filled with a year's worth of essays. Don't worry, replied another, just ask to see each draft of an essay as the student develops it. But then they'll offer their rough work and notes on disk along with the essays, fretted the first, determined to find reasons that students should have restricted access to a medium he himself had just discovered.

Despite its awkward interface and rough edges, The Electronic Village is crowded every night of the week, as teachers find their way into its discussion groups on their own time. Even with its provincewide scale, it is proving to be a valuable grass-roots experiment whose success is being driven by the enthusiasm of its users and their desire to share ideas and to learn new skills. And for many teachers, The Electronic Village is doing exactly what organizers hoped. Teachers discover a fascinating new realm of possibilities when they go online, and every good teacher, hungry for anything captivating to feed to his or her classroom of students, immediately wonders how this resource can be turned to the benefit of the kids. As similar projects spread across Canada, spurred on by the federal government's SchoolNet project, the majority of teachers who by nature are curious will find themselves unable to resist this pull into the information age.

Will Computers Ever Replace Teachers?

While teachers find that their role is changing considerably, it is unlikely that they will ever disappear. They were not replaced by the invention of the book or the telephone or even the television, and computers are not going to supplant them either. At best, the computer is a teacher's aide, capable of giving a lot of assistance to students and teachers alike, but that is where its power ends.

Meanwhile, teachers have begun to shed their role as authoritative expert and professional lecturer and have assumed the job of learning coach, resource coordinator and classroom animator. While old-time teachers were expected to know just about everything that a student needed to know, contemporary teachers are expected to know how to uncover information instead. There is less emphasis on drilling and more on discussion and exploration. Teachers now try to stimulate students to think for themselves and uncover knowledge by handling information.

Much of what computers do has little connection to actual teaching. Word processing software, for example, doesn't do anything until a student launches it and starts giving shape to his or her thoughts. Similarly, a spreadsheet operates as a tool that can be used for an almost infinite number of jobs, but the student generates the information by employing the program. The value of the computer in these cases is not that it imparts knowledge to the child but, rather, that it extends the student's abilities in the same manner that a pencil and notepad aid memory.

Of course, there are hundreds of programs that do stand

in for a teacher's assistant and supplement more traditional teaching methods. There are flashcard software packages, the drill-and-practice material that many people associate with educational computing; games and educational packages that encourage problem solving; and the informative disks and CDs that offer multimedia reference material. They have a place in schools; but they are not electronic teachers.

The image of a machine that disgorges knowledge into a child is not even very interesting science fiction anymore. Computers, like books, magazines, posters, group activities and field trips to the zoo, are a resource that works well in the hands of a skilled teacher and motivated students.

Do Teachers Need Their Own Computers?

After years of assuming that a school merely needed to be filled with computers to bring it into the information age, observers have recently come to the forehead-slapping conclusion that it is even more important for teachers to know how to operate them so that they can put the machines to use.

Recognizing this, some school boards in Canada and the United States are assigning computers to teachers rather than simply putting them into classrooms or labs for student use only. In retrospect, the wisdom of the idea seems obvious. Suddenly, the new computer is a carrot, presented as a helpful device capable of easing both administrative and teaching chores. Not only has the learn-it-or-else stick been put away, but the teacher has been given a head start on the kids who — as all adults ruefully acknowledge — peculiarly tend to become familiar with and embrace computers much faster than do their elders. Although it may seem an expensive gesture at first, school boards generally find that teachers are eager to find ways to make their workday and their off-hours' preparation time more efficient. If a teacher is convinced that a computer adds to that efficiency, then he or she is transformed into a highly motivated self-trainer instead of a reluctant employee who must be forced to attend training sessions.

Self-motivation, of course, is not enough by itself to turn teachers into computer users, but it is the most important first step in the training process. Teachers who take equipment home after work and on weekends have a chance to experiment with a variety of programs (including some addictive games, no doubt) and will feel their way toward developing their own uses. Keeping student records on data bases that provide easy overviews of a term's worth of assignments would appeal to some, while others would find it more useful to produce newsletters and printed classroom material. Eventually, the results of the computer-loan perk will find their way into the day-to-day curriculum, as teachers merge their newfound technical skills with their teaching techniques.

Isn't Money Too Tight to Offer Computers to Teachers?

Before dismissing this approach solely on the basis of money, school boards should consider the costs of *not* speeding up the use of computers by their teachers. To date, millions of dollars have been spent on equipment without a significant return on that investment; further computer purchases will only result in more waste if the issue of effective training continues to be ignored.

When accountants in a business take a close look at the real cost of buying a computer and software for an employee, they find that the initial price tag and financing charges make up only 17 percent of the real cost to the company. In 1993, according to an analysis by the Gartner Group of Stamford, Connecticut, the true cost of a single personal computer (spread over five years) ranged from $25,000 (for an Apple Macintosh) to $35,000 (for a personal computer with a DOS operating system). Training and support services represent about 12 percent of the five-year cost, while up to 57 percent is charged to the cost incurred while an employee learns how to use it. In other words, the largest cost factor is not in the purchase price but in the amount of downtime an employee has while he or she acquires a whole new set of job skills. (Not surprisingly, the report concluded that expensive computers which were easy to use saved a lot of money in the long run.)

With those statistics in mind, it is easy to see the benefits of encouraging teachers to start using computers at home on their own time, even if there is no budget for buying new computers right away. Employee payroll-deduction programs already exist within many school boards to ease the personal expense of a new computer, and both Apple and IBM offer substantial discounts to teachers and administrators who buy computers for educational uses.

Other low-cost plans could include free summer or

weekend training courses for school board employees and even a cash incentive to teachers who complete such a course and want to buy their own computer.

Near Ottawa, the Carleton Board of Education and the University of Ottawa have joined forces to offer three university credit courses in basic and advanced computer skills — all designed with the specific needs of Carleton Board teachers in mind. Even though the teachers have to pay $800 for the courses, enrollment is high. While the Board may eventually have to pay the course graduates higher salaries as their credits raise them to higher pay categories, it has saved in the long run by escaping the high cost of training staff on school time.

In some school districts, the issue of training is tied directly to the assignment of computers; a teacher can have a computer only if he or she also agrees to complete a specified number of hours of computer workshops within the next year or two. In Ontario, however, provincial funding for computers emphasizes the acquisition of the equipment and software. Teacher training is largely left to the local boards, and few of them have followed Carleton's lead in establishing adequate training and support programs.

So, Self-Instruction Is Not the Total Answer?

Supplying teachers with computers may spark their interest in using the machines in the classroom, but it is not reasonable to expect that teachers can quickly train themselves to a level at which they become qualified computer instructors. We don't expect teachers to be home-taught physicists or mathematicians, and there is no magic in the computer that replaces the need for giving teachers professional training for their new role. Putting a computer on a teacher's desk is only a start, and handled incorrectly, it can place enormous pressure on a teacher and undermine his or her confidence.

Ongoing training sessions not only increase the skill levels of the teachers but also provide a solid educational basis for computer use rather than abandoning the teacher to whatever logic he or she can wring out of the software itself. With a regular training program in place, new computer users get a good head start at classroom planning, while those with experience are able to keep current with emerging technology and fine-tune their skills. Intermittent (if not regular) training needs to be available for teachers at all levels, but the current organization of professional development (PD) days is probably inadequate — especially as school boards have begun to appropriate them for uses other than teacher education (such as parent-teacher interviews, disposable time in lieu of layoffs and year-end catch-up days). But there is also a need for some form of technical support available to teachers at all times to provide quick answers to minor queries and fast solutions to major technical malfunctions. After all, it is hard for teachers to plan lessons that include computer use if they are never sure whether the equipment can be trusted to run smoothly.

Most schools already have an arrangement with at least one computer-literate teacher on staff to serve as a computer resource person. The theory is that the more experienced teachers can provide encouragement and help

"So you tried to install some more RAM yourself, did you?"

to their peers. Sometimes, they are even given a slightly reduced teaching load to accommodate this function. Usually, though, they are an inadequate resource without enough time to service all of a school's needs. Their busiest time is typically in September, at the start of a new school year, when a dozen or more teachers are calling on them to pull computers out of storage and reestablish schoolwide networks. While other teachers spend a day or two arranging their classrooms for the first day, the computer-resource teacher needs several days to do everyone else's setup. Added to the frustrations of dealing with other people's problems and working overtime for free is the likelihood that the equipment is old and easily breaks down.

There are heroes, of course, who take on the challenges voluntarily and, in the right circumstance, can single-handedly lead an entire staff into the computer age with nothing more than enthusiasm and determination. One such fellow was a modest middle-aged teacher who still works for one of Ontario's separate school boards. Although the school had been given Macintosh computers for each of its classrooms some years before, the principal had decided that the computers were an irritant and had locked them up in storage where they "would be safe," although it was never clear who or what was at risk and where the danger was lurking. Upon the principal's retirement, Peter (as we shall call him for the purposes of this story) unofficially liberated the equipment and used his holiday time to set up a makeshift computer lab before the new principal arrived. Without any knowledge of networks and with only a basic understanding of computers, Peter got the computers up and running and taught himself enough to oversee the students' use of the equipment. He then began to recruit his fellow teachers, convincing them that this was technology worthy of their interest.

Peter was not totally successful, of course, but he did more in that year to implement the province's mandatory use of computers than his former principal had done during his career. Amazingly, he felt he had to sneak around behind the administration's back even though the equipment he used had been purchased and placed in his school by the local board.

What Other Kinds of Help Do Teachers Need?

Parents who have some experience with computers should offer teachers help when they need it. Community volunteers play an important part in many schools, providing library services, reading assistance and even in-class help. But not all teachers are good at asking for help, and a potential volunteer who simply says, "Call me if there is anything I can do" is unlikely to be called. If a parent has a skill to contribute, teachers usually prefer to hear about it and then find a way to apply it to something useful. Many school computers (even the antiquated ones) could be put to better use if someone had the time to read the manuals and find out what they can do. Teachers with a classroom full of children do not have the time to putter with obstinate machines but might be pleased to have the use of a computer that was resurrected. But volunteers should be prepared to follow up their technical contributions by spending time working at the computer with students on projects that fit in with the teacher's plan. There is no sense in setting up software that has no relevance to the class.

Bringing other parents on side in the technology debate is also important. Information sessions and computer open houses will ease the fears of many doubting parents who misunderstand the role of computers in the school. If interested parents and volunteers ignore this crucial step, then teachers will be left to defend a technology that they may not completely understand or agree with. Once dissenting parents get a whiff of uncertainty or pessimism, they can undo a lot of progress simply through their own ignorance of the issues.

Selfless acts of charity and generosity should be tempered by a realistic evaluation of what is needed. Busy teachers with no computer experience are not going to be ready for a complete makeover of their curriculum. Small steps are best at first. Parent support groups considering the donation of computer equipment should be sure also that their gifts match the needs of the school. One parent volunteer, a computer specialist from a university, recalls an eager bunch of parents who raised several thousand dollars to purchase a wonderful state-of-the-art desktop publishing system capable

"Personally, I'm delighted that you've come to believe in the value of computers, but can't you leave it at school?"

of producing outstanding material for staff and students. Unfortunately, nobody bothered to arrange for a good training program or volunteer operators or maintenance, and the staff guiltily put the equipment to one side, unable to take the time to learn how to use it. Without realizing what they had done, the helpful parents had put a lot of unnecessary pressure on the teachers, which in turn pushed them even further away from computers. Years later, the machine continues to collect dust and is seldom turned on, and the parents' group remains unhappy without understanding why its gift went unappreciated.

What Else Makes the Computer Transition Easier?

Consistency in planning and expectations at the school board level is a final important key to winning over teacher acceptance. School boards need to have very clear guidelines about their technological policies and how they expect change to be set in motion. Teachers who have been told to use computers for student word processing and for their own recordkeeping one year and are then told about a new emphasis on CD-ROM or network communications shortly after can be forgiven for being cynical about the quality of leadership.

Part of any implementation plan should include a decent policy on the question of what platform or type of computer hardware to use. Across both Canada and the United States, it is not unusual for schools to have a mishmash of conflicting equipment that can neither interconnect nor share software. Fifteen-year-old Commodore 64s, old Apple IIs,

ICONs and cheap clones can be found alongside more useful Macintoshes and IBM-style machines. As the latter two major companies (and several smaller ones using the same operating systems) are the driving force behind current technological standards, it makes sense for most boards to cut their losses and quit adding to their stock of nonstandard models. New software is being developed continually to allow for easier networking between Apple and IBM systems, but it remains an imperfect solution.

If one assumes that school boards are capable of choosing useful computer platforms which are easy to learn and easy to maintain, it makes sense that all their teachers use the same basic kind of equipment. That way, teachers transferring from one school to another (or even to a different classroom in the same school) will be able to use the existing equipment without having to begin the expensive training phase all over again. As well, students moving through the grades or to a different neighbourhood will find the computer part of the transition easier.

THE ADMINISTRATION

If you want to understand how decisions are made about your child's education, attend a couple of local school board meetings. In theory, school boards are the perfect model of grass-roots democracy: the members are ordinary folks with real jobs elsewhere; they perform all their official duties right in the communities that elected them; and their decisions directly affect their neighbours' wallets and children. But while the pure democratic nature of it all can be exhilarating, it can also be sobering to consider that these ordinary folks — some of whom are creative geniuses, while others tend toward paranoia and curmudgeonliness — are setting the tone for our children's education. And spending millions of dollars doing it.

There are controls, of course, but the system seems based on some zany military hierarchy in which the strategic plans from the generals in the provincial capital are executed by a merry band of volunteer officers who sometimes don't reissue the orders to the front-line troops. In 1992, for example, when the Ontario government ordered all its school boards to provide a specific amount of computer time to every student in its jurisdiction, most of the boards simply accepted the message but did not act upon it. "We have limited weapons for the attack," they reasoned, "so we will just sit tight until the top brass sends us some more money." The battle for technological superiority in those schools was lost for lack of local leadership.

Money, of course, is the problem for most school boards. Up to 95 percent of a local budget may be made up of fixed costs such as salaries and mortgages, leaving lots of room for debate but little else. The only sources for additional funds are usually the provincial government (grants issued for specific sorts of projects) and municipal tax increases, which means that budgeting tends to be centred around cost-cutting and reallocation of limited money. It is no wonder that low-cost/high-profile issues such as school behaviour codes and literacy (or the perceived lack thereof) receive so much attention.

In recent years, those money problems have only gotten worse as provincial budgets are cut. As a result, boards have entirely lost their ability to make long-range plans for computerization or anything else, because no school board can count on enough money being allotted from year to year to carry out future phases of a plan. In 1984, for instance, Ontario started giving local school boards large annual grants to buy computers and many boards drew up strategies, but that money was cut in half before schools had been able to set up realistic technology programs. Schools in the other provinces across Canada suffered the same fate.

Given the tight money situation, local boards are hard-pressed to meet the demands of their constituents. But as any parent knows, school boards can be pressured to loosen up funds for programs if enough noise is created around an issue. After all, no school board has a perfect budget, and finding money for computers and training is sometimes simply a matter of being creative and reassessing the value of services and traditional approaches to day-to-day operations. The annual cost of running a school board courier service in a rural system (complete with trucks and drivers), for example, could be drastically reduced (and even improved) if internal memos and teaching material were delivered by a combination of computer networks and private couriers. Or individual schools could be told that they each have to find room in their individual budgets for one or more additional computers each year but that it was up to the principal and the teachers and the parents (maybe even the students) to figure out how to do it.

However, before the creative accounting and budgeting can take place, there must be the political will to prepare for the computer age. The public and its school board trustees must be committed to making changes, and a careful look at those elected faces around a meeting table will give a parent clues as to how prepared these pillars of the community are to take the local kids into the 21st century.

Where Does Computer Money Come From?

Theoretically, it is simple: school boards fulfill the educational requirements of their province using a combination of provincial grants and local money to do so. When it comes to computers, the province may set standards (2.5 hours a week per student and 1 computer for every 10 students in Ontario) and may also offer ways to ease the cost of such requirements with grant money. It is up to the local boards to take the money and meet the standards.

In Ontario, annual grants are offered through the Grant Eligible Microcomputers (GEMs) process, which to date is responsible for financing two-thirds of the province's 180,000 classroom computers. The program was launched in 1984, when there was only 1 computer per 39 schoolchildren; that ratio is currently at about 1:11. It was an ambitious program at first that saw roughly $50 million to $60 million go to school boards each year, but the annual total has dwindled steadily toward the $20 million range in recent years. Interestingly, though, GEMs money was meant to supplement local funding rather than replace it, and each board had to submit a computer-implementation plan as part of its annual GEMs application.

Actually, the original GEMs program was not as educational as its boosters might have suggested, for it was part of an early-eighties industrial strategy designed to launch Ontario's own homegrown high-tech Silicon Valley. In 1984, when the first GEMs money was awarded, school boards could use it only to buy the ICON computer, a made-in-Ontario technical wonder designed specifically for educational use. At the time, the ICON was considered very advanced, and its most noticeable feature, a tracker ball to one side of the keyboard, allowed the user to move the on-screen cursor without having to type commands through the keyboard. It also had a colour monitor. Not only was it going to create jobs for Ontario, it was going to make kids love computers. (The fact that the ICON shares the same birth year as Apple's revolutionary and very successful Macintosh

"No, you idiot, she wants the answer rounded off to the nearest one-millionth."

system, complete with its mouse and idiotproof user interface, is certainly ironic.)

The launch of the ICON failed for a number of reasons, but its biggest problems were that teachers never received enough training to make full use of the technology and that its developers were unable to match the innovations of the mainstream computer world, where companies had to fight for market share. While the major computer companies were making their computers faster and easier to use, the ICON lagged further and further behind. Teachers who knew a lot about computers tended to dismiss ICONs as primitive, and teachers who knew nothing about computers had a hard time figuring them out at all. And, because every computer in a school was hooked into a precarious ICON network, when one of the machines failed, it took everything else down with it.

By 1989, development on the ICON had stopped; the new model was simply a middle-of-the-road computer (made by Intel) in an ICON III case. It operated like an IBM computer but could also run the old, kludgy ICON software that dated back to 1984. Amazingly, Ontario (the ICON's only real customer) has purchased 63,000 ICONs in total, and Unisys, the American company that now owns the ICONIX name, still provides about 35 percent of the computers bought by Ontario schools each year.

Sadly, the government created few permanent jobs with the $400 million worth of GEMs grants to date (the ICON jobs were moved to South Korea in 1986, throwing the company's Brockville, Ontario, employees out of work), and the

ICON/GEMs policy actually managed to retard the use of computers in the schools for several years. By the time other, more advanced and accessible products were deemed eligible for GEMs money, every school board in the province had already committed to ICON technology, and many were reluctant to switch to different computer platforms even though IBM machines became GEMs-eligible as early as 1988. Today, Apple, Olivetti, Commodore and a few clone makers have also been granted GEMs status, but despite its limitations, the ICON remains the computer of choice in many boards — not because it is state of the art but because they have always bought ICONs and to change now would mean starting all over again. The attraction of the ICON is not what it can do in the future but, rather, its peculiar links with Ontario's recent past.

The parent company, Unisys, sells state-of-the-art Intel computers to schools in Prince Edward Island and New Brunswick and provides educational consulting services all around the world. Aside from a small testing project in South Africa, however, it does not even try to sell the ICON outside Ontario.

In those provinces not affected by the ICON experiment, schools are faced with the old Apple II. These educational computers, designed by the same Apple computer company that later introduced the Macintosh, were intended to become a powerful standard of educational computing. Tens of thousands of the machines ended up in schools all over North America, and although the company supported them for a few years and brought out subsequent generations of machines, it abandoned the whole line in 1983, ending that particular evolution of hardware and software and leaving the Apple IIs to rot. This policy outraged many customers, but at least it had the effect of forcing school boards to face reality and switch to more modern types of computers. (Unfortunately, the experience left many purchasers unhappy and dampened enthusiasm for Apple's Macintosh — a line that is well suited to novice users.)

Besides the ICON and Apple II, there are many other outdated machines in schools, such as early Radio Shack (Tandy) models and Commodore 64s, and none of these represent the same kind of open path to future technologies as the newer Macintosh and IBM-style DOS-based computers. In fact, they are all technological dead ends.

Do Governments Buy Software Too?

Along with the GEMs control of hardware, the Ontario government maintained a similar influence on the software decisions of local boards. An initiative called the Ontario Educational Software Service (OESS) oversaw the distribution of software that was tailored to the Ontario curriculum and underwritten by provincial grants. This produced a flurry of simple programs in the mid-eighties, most of them designed by moonlighting teachers, but there was not a big enough market for ICON software to attract major investment by mainstream developers. As a result, the Ontario strategy did little to help create a homegrown software industry.

During the early ICON years, the OESS was intended to pay for newly created software, but since then, the program has changed. Now the service purchases provincewide licences for existing commercial software and makes it available to school boards without additional cost to them. Similar organizations exist for the other provinces, and these have the effect of making some very good — and costly — programs and applications available to every school at no charge. Although much of the material comes from large American developers, more Canadian software is being produced now by companies that know they can design with local school systems in mind and then adapt products for the United States and other countries.

Why Do Some Boards Support Computers?
Money, as we have already seen, is a major factor in a school board's use of computers. But attitude is also a key element. Until local politicians and their senior administrators develop an understanding of why computers are needed in schools and how to place them there effectively, money alone is not going to help.

John Beaver, an educational technology professor at the State University of New York at Buffalo, believes that the attitudes of senior managers in school systems are preventing the spread of effective computer education. He points to a study of western New York State in 1992 in which he found that 41 percent of responding educators felt their schools' planning process was dictated by senior management. "Educational leaders," he observes, "are the neck of the hourglass that is separating teachers from resources. We need our leaders to see themselves as the pilots who will guide the development of their instructional technology programs."

Beaver believes that the improvement of school technology curricula will not come until more administrators learn the basics of computers themselves and start to use them on a daily basis. Right now, his studies from west-central Florida and New York State suggest that as many as 73 percent of administrators felt they had no personal competence on computers. Interestingly, 62 percent admitted that they thought the quality of their schools' technology programs was unsatisfactory.

There are, of course, some boards in which strong,

"I don't know what the thing does, but we probably can't ignore it much longer."

consistent leadership has produced amazingly effective approaches to computer education, but they are rare exceptions. One is the Carleton Board of Education that manages the school district which surrounds (but does not include) the city of Ottawa. The Carleton Board has very aggressive purchasing and training policies that make it one of the most technologically advanced administrations in Canada, and it has not relied on provincial funds or policies to fuel its approach. In fact, the main reason for its success is its local citizenry. Responsible for education in the sprawling suburbs that have grown up around the capital, the Carleton Board has been encouraged to act progressively by its taxpayers, which include well-paid government managers, computer-literate civil servants and the work force of the region's high-tech industry.

Why Has the Carleton Board Succeeded?

The region has both the political will for technological change and a solid tax base, which is an excellent — and rare — combination. While many Canadian school boards have pilot projects and showcase schools, the Carleton Board has graduated to a full-blown implementation stage.

Certainly, the overall attitude toward technology at all levels of the Board stands out. Everyone seems either to share the Board's pro-computer attitude or at least to be very aware of it. There are still skeptics, of course, but generally, the Carleton Board has created a healthy climate for change, in which teachers are encouraged to avail themselves of the resources they need to improve their use of computers in the classroom. To some degree or other, there is commitment at all levels, from the public, trustees and supervisors all the way through to the extensive support staff, the 3,500 teachers and the 46,000 students themselves. The question of whether to have computers has long since been answered, and the focus now is on the more interesting matters of how to make computers useful and how to get the most computer service for every dollar spent.

The high levels of participation within the Carleton Board point to a coordinated effort that reaches out from the central office. While most school boards have office space set aside for the computer personnel that run the administration's big mainframe computers, that space in the Carleton Board offices is matched, if not surpassed, by the offices of a staff dedicated to the distribution and maintenance of microcomputers in the schools.

In the 1994-95 school year, the 39-member computer department staff included:

• 5 full-time repair technicians to fix school computers as well as update facilities and improve network wiring

• 4 support staff to train secretaries and office personnel

• 2 support staff to train teachers

• 2 computer system designers

• 2 network experts who oversee classroom networks

• 2 teachers (one high school, one elementary) assigned to provide support to teachers and to conduct workshops

• 1 teacher who acts as a full-time consultant seconded to the Carleton Board office to oversee support services

This whole group exists to remove obstacles from the

path of teachers who want to teach their students to use computers in the Board's 38 schools. In practical terms, the extraordinary level of technical support helps avoid all the class-stopping frustrations that plague so many schools when systems crash and can't be fixed, but it also sends a strong message that the Board is committed to making computers work for teachers and kids. The moment a teacher shows interest in using computers or has a problem, he or she gets both encouragement and resources.

Throughout the Carleton Board, each school has a staff member who serves as a computer contact person and attends monthly meetings to keep abreast of the latest available resources. Any teacher who has begun using computers with his or her class and who encounters a problem can turn to more experienced people on staff, including the computer contact teacher, and if the school's in-house means fail, then he or she can be referred to one of the two Special Assignment Teachers (SATs) at the Board office.

The SATs are regular classroom teachers receiving a full salary while they serve two-year terms at the Board office. They take on any computer problem that a classroom teacher experiences. This can be a simple matter of describing shortcuts or particular commands within applications or warning teachers away from software conflicts or may involve explaining the intricacies of a network configuration. In addition, SATs provide more academic advice on integrating the available computer resources into classroom activities. A mathematics teacher who already knows about MathBlaster and other educational games but is looking for something more sophisticated can turn to the SATs for advice on using spreadsheets. A geography teacher can learn the easiest way to search the existing resources for computerized topographical maps or can simply get a run-down of the available resources around which particular classes and new teaching units can be organized.

When they are not troubleshooting or providing advice, the SATs evaluate new software, both the programs licensed by the provincial government and materials that come directly to the Board from retailers. Even if the software is not covered by a provincial licence, there are funds set aside to buy or license useful software for the Carleton Board.

The SATs also devote time to the evangelical task of convincing more teachers to acquire computer literacy. There are still a relatively large number of teachers who haven't had time to learn about the computers or who simply don't want to, so the SATs conduct regular workshops to encourage their co-workers to take advantage of the Board's resources. In this, they are like librarians who tell everyone about the latest books on the shelves — with the difference that sometimes, they must also explain how to get that book down from the shelf and find the first page. They are the connection between teachers on the one hand and all the expertise in the Board office on the other.

How Can Boards Make Computerization Easier?

While most school boards have a hodgepodge collection of different kinds of computers, the Carleton Board has proved the value of using a single platform for all its schools. (Platform refers to the basic software that operates a computer, known as system software. The most common system software programs are DOS and Windows for IBM-style machines and the graphical Macintosh system developed by Apple.)

Choosing a single platform, of course, does have its setbacks, particularly when the one selected becomes a dead-end technology, as was the case with the ICON. But given the current state of personal computers and the new degree of cooperation between IBM and Apple, it is much safer now for school boards to choose one platform than it was earlier in the history of computer development.

The Carleton Board chose the Macintosh computer platform in the eighties and has stuck with its decision even though there are perennial suggestions that the schools should align themselves more closely with the business world, where DOS and Windows machines still predominate. The arguments for and against any particular platform are best left for individual boards to debate (although the authors, who both use Macintosh systems, admit to a bias for Apple computers and prefer them for their fairly foolproof interfaces and tolerance of technical blundering).

Some observers maintain that kids learning about computers benefit most when they work on a haphazard assortment of machines. Even though all computers process information by manipulating binary code, different brands of computers run on different operating systems and use different commands or even radically different kinds of commands. Theoretically, a certain logic flows from the fundamental nature of the technology, and children learning how to use several kinds of machines acquire a generic level of understanding that makes them better learners of computer skills. Some call this the computing school of hard knocks.

On the other hand, a single platform means that as children move through the grades, they build on each year's experience and are able to become extremely sophisticated users of the software they master. This obviously makes life easier for teachers and students alike. Carleton's determination to stick with the Macintosh system, which generally remains less common in the work world than its competitors, has proved useful for a number of reasons, and criticism has died down over the years — especially as computer systems have all become more alike.

For a school board's technical department, the advantages of the single platform are clear: technicians need only learn the peculiarities of one brand; they establish relationships with their counterparts at the manufacturer, and they do so as an extremely valuable customer, rather than as someone who does not know where next year's budget is going. After a training period, Apple even allows the Carleton Board technicians to perform warranty repair work, saving the time required to ship equipment back and forth to the manufacturers.

Having technicians trained by Apple gives Carleton a clearer idea of the capabilities of the machines and frees its purchasing department from relying only on salespeople for information about new equipment — which is continually being considered, because the Board replaces all equipment more than seven years old.

A single platform greatly simplifies the Board's responsibility for coordinating and encouraging computer use in all its schools. Teacher and student training is made easier, especially as each school gains additional expertise with every new user. Classroom teachers benefit not only because of this shared expertise within a school but also because it makes transfer between schools (by staff and students) much easier.

By sticking with one kind of computer, a board also manages to coordinate the efforts of the community and parents groups, ensuring that donations fit in with the overall plans of the board and the schools.

How Should Computers Be Allocated?

Sometimes the people who need the most help are also the most reluctant to ask for it, a problem that many school boards have failed to address. When computers are being handed out, they are usually either shared among teachers equally (the equity approach) or given to those who can best articulate how they need them (the bidding approach).

Both systems have their drawbacks. The first means that brand-new computers may sit unused because teachers do not know how (or do not want) to use them. Better training is the only solution to that dilemma, and it is expensive.

The bidding system presents a more serious dilemma. For boards that want to get maximum use out of scarce resources, this may be an easy solution, but it creates a whole new problem, because it severely limits the number of computer users in a school system and stifles the spread of computer skills to untrained teachers. If a new CD-ROM arrives in the library, the teacher who knows the most about software is probably the one who will use it the most. When limited staff training is made available, the computer-literate teachers often attend the sessions. If a machine is sitting idle somewhere, a teacher who knows how to use it is far likelier to get his or her hands on it.

In the end, the equity approach is probably much more effective at integrating computers throughout schools, but it is also more expensive at first because of the added cost of training. Many boards which are image-conscious may also find that the equitable distribution of computers severely limits the sex appeal of their technological showplaces; equity tends to highlight how thinly existing resources are spread.

Should Computers Be Put in Classrooms or Labs?

Parents who begin to ask questions about computers quickly come upon the "lab versus classroom" debate. The question has been around since the seventies: if there are 30 machines, should there be 3 in each of 10 classes or should they be lined up row upon row in a single room? It is an issue that once turned on the more strictly academic concern about whether kids should be seated in a room full of computers and have basic skills drilled into them or whether they should encounter the machines in the classroom and be encouraged to view them as part of the learning environment.

Today, however, the question of where to put a school's computers involves a number of less dramatic-sounding issues. Most are practical concerns that can be decided only on a school-by-school basis. If the teachers in a school are not generally well trained in the use of computers, then a computer lab supervised by someone who is experienced works much better. A good lab person can be the same kind of resource as a skilled librarian, guiding students in their use of the machines and helping teachers keep track of what's available. Eventually, as skills improve, those computers can find their way back into the classrooms.

Even when teachers do possess the necessary training, a lab may be necessary to ease the sharing of limited equipment, and in the case of schools with temperamental machines, labs can ease the crisis presented by periodic breakdowns that can leave some classes without access to machines for days on end.

On the other hand, if skilled teachers are well supported, then placing computers in classrooms has the decided advantage of providing constant access. Children can be shown by example that the computer is a tool with numerous applications. They can be taught how to make computing a natural part of learning rather than experiencing the machines as something that one uses only during scheduled periods. This approach is probably more in keeping with current thought on how to blend computers with the existing curriculum.

Increasingly, both options are being used. Some machines go into labs, others into classrooms; and in some schools, teachers from three or four classes pool their resources and set up a few machines as a computer "pod" where they can send groups of kids to work on special assignments.

Will Computers Be Stolen?

Security is another of those practical issues that intrude on the debate about where to put the machines. In some schools, especially at the secondary level, not only will there be kids who know more about running the equipment than their parents and teachers, a few will also know exactly how to open up the computer case to get at all sorts of expensive parts, from memory chips and hard drives to modems. Chaining the equipment to a table doesn't prevent this kind of unauthorized modification, so in some schools, the high-powered new machines go into labs where they can be better supervised; only the older units that aren't worth disembowelling are distributed to classes.

There are other security issues as well. Software licensed to the school can be stolen by simply inserting a disk and copying the program; illegal software can be copied onto the school's system, which, in theory at least, exposes the school to prosecution. With so many users, a school's system is vulnerable to computer viruses, and as schools hook up to the Internet, there is the highly publicized concern that kids will be using school machines to share pornography and to discuss inappropriate subjects. All of these, however, are practical matters that must be handled as issues of student behaviour and discipline. After all, no one argues that soccer should be avoided in schools because students can steal the balls, and by the same token, security issues must be kept in perspective in discussions of computer implementation.

What Role Do Principals Play?

Any parent who has the pleasure of seeing a good principal at work knows how important such a person can be in building a team of teachers who share common goals and receive a lot of encouragement. A principal should be capable of leading his or her staff through tough times, and the introduction of computers into a school certainly qualifies as that.

Principals receive direction from Board of Education officials and run schools along lines laid down at the Board and Ministry of Education levels. However, a principal also budgets money and schedules time within a school and, by encouraging or discouraging teachers, can profoundly affect how staff members work. During this time, then,

"Don't worry, we'll have graduated before the teacher even notices it isn't working."

when expectations of how computers will be used in schools are often so ambiguous, principals can be either strong forces for change or bottlenecks in the system. By simply doing nothing, a principal can slow matters to a stop.

Some boards with limited computer budgets have experimented by giving principals computers to ease their administrative tasks and have found that once these principals learn the value of the equipment, they become very creative in finding ways to integrate the machines into everyday school life.

Leadership from principals depends on everything from their personalities to the extent that they were already using computer technology in their positions as administrators. But once principals are committed to computer implementation, there are numerous ways they can speed things along. They have a role in fund-raising, and they can motivate teachers with simple encouragement and by arranging professional development time. They can give priority to scheduling computer time for classes, and they can build parental interest into effective support. They are also in a position to assess what's going on in the school as a whole and to ensure that the momentum for this process of change is maintained.

How Can School Boards Be Encouraged to Computerize?
While trustees and administrators are fairly accessible to parents, sometimes more than gentle persuasion is necessary to win over support for change, so it is wise to have a basic understanding of what provincial educational guidelines require.

140

Every school board has to have a core curriculum document that outlines, grade by grade, what skills are to be taught in every subject. Whether or not schools actually have the necessary equipment to support the curriculum, there is an official plan that does require the teaching of computer skills, if not the integration of those skills into other subject areas. These curriculum documents are periodically reviewed and updated by both local superintendents and Ministry officials so that they meet provincial standards. All teachers and principals are supposed to base their teaching on these guidelines, and copies should be available at board offices.

Provincial governments also should have current guidelines for the way computers are to be used. While premiers and ministers of education tend to speak glowingly of their own efforts at preparing children for the information age, much of the rhetoric falls flat in the face of the working documents that govern the school system.

In Ontario, the 1992 Policy/Program Memorandum Number 116 sets out numerous computer requirements:

"School boards are responsible for developing flexible long-term plans for the integration of computers into the curriculum.

The plan shall outline strategies for:

• the integration of computers into all areas of the curriculum in all schools;

• the development of learning objectives for the use of computers in all grades and in all areas of the curriculum;

• the sharing of curriculum resources among schools,

divisions, departments and teachers."

Policy/Program Memorandum Number 116 requires that a board's plan address issues of "equitable access for all students to the use of computers in the classroom," professional development for teachers, ongoing support services, acquisition of resources and equipment, special education needs and evaluation and coordination of planning at the school level.

The memorandum also specifically requires that the board's plan address the need to consult and share information with parents and community members and to "work with parents and community members to plan for the use of computers in meeting the needs of all students."

In Ontario, then, parents are required players in the process of putting computers in schools, and in practice, that probably means a determined individual could find a seat on a committee.

All school boards in Ontario were required to submit their computer implementation plans to the government by May 1994 or face reduced provincial funding for computers. In addition, boards and individual schools were subject to random audits by the Ministry to ensure that they were putting these plans into action. In fact, however, in 1994, there was only one person to conduct the audits of the province's 128 school boards, and the Ministry's threat of reduced grants carried little weight, as it would have meant reducing the purchase of computers by the boards that were most in need of them. In practice, even schools that failed miserably to meet the minimum standards survived the audit process if their principals were able to write a convincing computer plan — regardless of whether a lack of equipment made such a plan meaningless.

How Can Parents Become Directly Involved?

The school board as a whole, of course, does not concern itself solely with matters of learning. Generally, education (or curriculum or programming) is dealt with by one committee that reports back to the board of trustees along with several others, including Finance, Personnel and Transportation. Subcommittees of the education committee deal with such issues as prayer in schools and sex education, and it is at this level that one will most likely find a group of people — trustees, school board employees, community members — grappling with the problems of computer implementation. One or two interested parents or community representatives can probably join such a subcommittee, and it is there that they can make direct arguments for particular policies.

Participation on a committee is no guarantee of any changes or improvements, as the true day-to-day decision making within a school board rests with the superintendents who supervise principals and with the director of education, highly paid professional administrators who can, and typically do, powerfully influence the actions of the elected board. Board trustees often find themselves rubber-stamping their senior staff's recommendations on the principle that these employees know what is best for education (which is often the case, but not always). Parents who find themselves on subcommittees which do not include a senior administrator can safely conclude that the panel is toothless and that its suggestions can be easily dismissed by the director of education, even though he or she may not have a clue as to the reasons behind a recommendation. If senior members do not attend committee meetings, then it is important to have the situation rectified — if only on the chance that someone in authority may actually learn about the matters being discussed.

While staff members of subcommittees tend to avoid confrontation with administrators, community members are more independent and have the option of making a presentation or an appeal directly to the trustees. Thus in a situation where the director of education or the superintendents may suggest that they have the support of a subcommittee, trustees can be told differently. One of the most effective defences against stonewalling administrators is a trustee meeting packed with dozens of concerned parents who make it clear by their mood that they are unhappy.

The Home Front

It seems clear that parents who are counting on schools to teach their kids about computers are courting disappointment, and many parents end up feeling that the easiest solution to the dilemma is to bring a computer home for the family to use, hoping it will supplement whatever meagre resources are found at the neighbourhood school. This is obviously an expensive response (and should not be seen as a solution to the school problem), but it is also an increasingly popular one — especially for high-income families. Statistics show that 66 percent of families earning $70,000 a year own at least one computer, and those percentages of ownership rise dramatically as income rises. Needless to say, the reverse is also true — low-income families have far fewer computers, and there is a danger that a lot of children will be deprived of computer-assisted learning for several more years if the school system is not reformed now.

Income alone, though, is probably not the driving force

behind the growing trend toward family computers. Certainly, $2,000 to $3,000 of disposable savings helps get a computer through the door, but an appreciation for the uses of the machines is also a big factor. Family members who use a computer at work (or at school) are likely to promote the purchase of one more vigorously than people who never use them. And a computer in the home of an experienced user is likely to see more use than one bought by a parent who has no idea how to use the machine. Parents who decide to introduce a computer to the home front are well advised to plan the purchase carefully and to be prepared to become personally involved in its use. They are also well advised to budget time to spend at the computer with their children. Children who read with their parents do better at school, and the same is likely true of computers.

Who Will Teach Our Children to Use a Home Computer?
With a little guidance, many children will teach themselves a lot simply through trial and error. Most adults who have watched kids use computers know that children tend to be fearless to the point of recklessness as they experiment, while adults may be too cautious, fearing that one false move will destroy their mysterious, expensive new machine. Enthusiastic kids will busily type in unfamiliar commands and trigger unknown options just out of curiosity. A modern brand-name computer is pretty resilient to freewheeling operators, so short of physical violence, there is probably not a lot to worry about as kids switch endlessly between games and applications. Worried parents can ease their own

fears by installing a program to limit a child's access to certain parts of the computer. This can protect sensitive computer files (such as family budgets and the system software that controls the operation of the computer) while establishing clear limits for the children to explore.

How Can I Help If I Don't Know What to Do?

Like teachers, parents can't be expected to know everything about computers. They just have to be willing to experiment

"Actually, I can't do the dishes tonight because I have to log onto a forum on Asian agrarian reform in fifteen minutes...and Bart Simpson starts at eight."

and do a bit of reading. As novices gain computer experience, they will eventually recognize the logic hidden within good software and begin to apply their new lessons to other problems. That process of simply getting a sense of how things work is more important than memorizing commands. That is why a child's haphazard approach is actually a good one to imitate.

A computer is a major purchase, but unlike a new car, it won't get wrecked easily. When you mess up on a test drive at your desk, no one gets hurt, nothing is scratched and your insurance rates don't rise. You just turn off the computer and start over again. Give your children lots of opportunity to experiment as well, and try not to let your nervousness get in the way.

Having multiple users around one computer at the same time makes sense at home, especially during the exploration stage of computing. After all, computers (like video games and television sets) should not be used as surrogate playmates, so take advantage of the early part of the learning curve to spend some time working with your children. Although an adult, loaded down with manuals and an innate fear of the unknown, may have trouble keeping up with a rambunctious child, both participants will learn more together than they will alone.

Involving experienced friends and neighbours makes a lot of sense, but even without such a handy resource, there are hundreds of books available to guide computer users through every possible predicament and software program. Publishers discovered some time ago that computer manuals are often difficult to penetrate, and they have made millions preparing third-party instruction books that may or may not be authorized by software developers. There are also instructional videotapes and even CD-ROM packages that offer step-by-step instructions.

New users should avoid complicated software in the early stages. Many computers come with a basic word processing program and perhaps even graphics and spreadsheet software. Buy a couple of good games to go with it, and make the early sessions as easy and fun as possible. If you have friends who know what they are doing, then consider their advice so that you can start with programs that they know well.

What Equipment Should I Buy?

Talk to your friends and family before choosing a particular kind of computer, but take their advice with a grain of salt. Their needs may be much different than yours, and the chances are that if they have had a machine for a few years, their equipment is a generation or two behind the current crop of products anyway.

The main choice is between the IBM world and the Apple Macintosh world, and while Macintosh users (these two authors included) tend to be evangelistic about their brand because of its shorter learning curve and because it operates all software along very predictable lines, the advent of new software systems from the giant Microsoft corporation and IBM itself means that the distinction is fading. Try the various options in the showroom, and choose the one you will learn more quickly.

Beware of really cheap IBM clones, however, and don't shop on the basis of price alone. Stick with the major brands (look for the expensive ads everywhere — Compaq, Toshiba, Intel, et cetera), and be cautious when someone tries to sell you a no-name computer that "will run like an IBM but at half the price." All software developers test their new programs on the mainstream makes and, in theory, will not release software until it works reliably on them. Cheap components and shabby assembly jobs plague the low end

"But, Mom, he's so friendly. And after I learn how to care for him, I promise to teach you too."

of the price scale and can discourage newcomers.

While built-in CD-ROM readers may be a good investment for families that want to be able to use reference works or complicated games, other peripherals like modems are best delayed until a new user has enough computer experience to feel comfortable checking out online services and the Internet.

Finally, do not put extra pressure on yourself by purchasing a computer close to a project deadline. Family budgets, income tax season and school assignments all cause enough stress on their own and do not need the extra pressure of a new computer to add to the chaos. Give yourself several months to learn your way around a system before you have to become productive.

What About Computer Training?
Many colleges and local night schools offer classes that can be well suited for the user who really needs a structured approach to learning. Most courses concentrate on IBM-style computers, given their business-school traditions, and there are far fewer courses for Macintosh users (although Apple might argue that such courses are not necessary because of its intuitive interface).

Children's training programs should be approached more cautiously, and parents should ask detailed questions about the kind of instruction being offered.

FutureKids (a chain of franchises found throughout Canada and the United States), for example, does not attempt to teach a set of job skills or the intricacies of either

Macintosh or IBM systems. Rather, it aims to provide kids with a generic understanding of computers and enough of a foundation that they are able to ignore the differences. Kids work on a great variety of software, using programs that are rotated regularly before students develop specific habits and get stuck on single techniques.

The FutureKids program also works on cognitive skills, critical thinking and team learning; it teaches kids that they don't have to be good at math in order to make a computer serve them well. Kids are encouraged to explore the machines and to find unexpected solutions to problems and to employ creative thinking skills. These are all valuable aspects of computer literacy and probably have a place in any commercial course or computer camp or special event. The important thing, however, is that any good program will have instructors who can explain their methods in similarly straightforward terms so that noncomputer users can judge what is being offered.

CONCLUSIONS

There seem to be so many things wrong with the state of computers in the Canadian public school system that it is almost too discouraging to contemplate. With approximately 5.4 million students in the system, the country probably needs almost 300,000 new computers to supplement the usable machines now in schools. In our deficit-ridden economy, that represents an investment of $600 million just so that every 10 children can have access to one basic computer in their classrooms.

Yet we are probably better off not thinking of computers in terms of hundreds of millions of dollars. After all, the most heartening successes of the past 10 years have been those that were initiated by individual teachers and principals rather than large bureaucracies; those parents who are interested in improving this aspect of our schools are best to just start at the classroom and work their way up through the system.

A good first step is to talk to your children to find out what their attitude is toward computers and school. If the class actually uses the machines as part of its daily curriculum, discuss how they are used. If the teacher provides a variety of computer activities, then it is safe to assume that your child is in good hands. If computer usage is spotty or nonexistent or emphasizes only technical skills, it is time to take a closer look.

Ask the teacher, in a nonthreatening way, whether computers are part of his or her regular classroom activities, and be prepared to request a demonstration of some of the software the children use. Enquire about the effectiveness of the equipment, and try to get a sense of the amount of support the school offers its staff in the use of computers. If the computer you are shown looks old, runs slowly and uses software that seems dated, then you may be looking at one of the 50 percent of school computers which are obsolete. If the teacher seems bewildered by the sudden interest in computers and is not able to answer your questions, take the time to explain your concern and ask the teacher whether he or she would like to join you in approaching the principal in order to pursue the matter further.

It is important at every stage of this process to keep the mood positive. Teachers and principals should feel that your interest is supportive and helpful rather than accusatory. Given the voluntary nature of the work to be done, everyone involved should feel excited and enthusiastic rather than resentful. Find out what works well, and then build on those strengths; do not just dig for negative things to complain about. Educators are accustomed to endless complaints and will be tempted to tune out complainers.

Make sure the principal is on side, because he or she is the school's team leader and this is a task that needs leadership by example rather than bullying. If the principal is uninterested or noncooperative, try to skirt the problem by subtly looking for a vice principal or teacher to lead the staff instead.

An interest in computers is not unusual in the nineties, so don't be shy about wanting information about the school's computer policies. If the school has an active parents group, you might ask for an information night where teachers and even board administrators can explain how children are using modern technology in their everyday work. If there is little or no computer usage throughout the school, suggest that the principal help organize a technology committee made up of teachers, parents and community members to try to assess the current state of the school's resources, both human and machine. In order to educate that committee, study the board's core curriculum documents to find out what teachers are expected to be doing with computers, and given that there is probably an official plan for computer use, try to find out what the roadblocks are to its implementation.

The most common reasons for noncomputer use will be a lack of training and inappropriate computers. Classroom volunteers who can find time to sort out the mysteries of existing machines and software will be a godsend to a teacher who does not have time during the day to mess around with computers. If the volunteers can get a few simple programs running at a classroom work centre, they can begin to show the teacher how the equipment works. Just make sure that the content is relevant to the classroom teaching plan. And keep everything related to the computer easy.

Even old computers should have some useful application, but broken equipment — or no equipment — is a real problem and requires work on two fronts, the first of which is the school board. Contact the main office technical department to try to remedy maintenance problems. If there are not enough computers to go around, then make enquiries to both board administrators and trustees about new equipment. Given the slow speed that such administrative wheels turn, you should also approach the second front — the parents and local community — for help.

First of all, the parents and teachers must be convinced that computers are a worthy addition to the school. An enthusiastic group of parents can accomplish a great deal, but before anything else, a parents group needs a plan of attack which is manageable and useful and which looks to the future. Aiming at buying three computers a year for the next 10 years is admirable, but there must also be a plan to arrange for the training of staff and students, maintenance agreements with the board technicians or local companies and an implementation plan that will see the machines put to good use. Sometimes, reality will dictate that one computer at a time, at least in the beginning, is simply more sensible than three at a time.

Any group donating equipment should be aware of some of the administrative issues involved. The local school board has the right to determine what kinds of computers can be given to schools, and if it has chosen the wrong platform for its schools, then it is up to the volunteers to change policy before making purchases. As well, equipment will probably become the property of the board, which means that agree-

"I'm going to call your teacher tomorrow. You seem to be doing all your homework these days, and frankly, I'm suspicious."

ments will have to be in place to make sure the computers stay in the schools which bought them and also that the donated equipment does not reduce the number of board-sponsored computers that are placed in the schools.

If a school board is reluctant to improve the use of computers in classrooms, parents will have to become more politically active. Stubborn or disinterested administrators may suddenly become more amenable to change once trustees start to support concerned parents. A community group that has the facts about its local school's inadequate equipment and the provincial government curriculum regulations would be well advised to present its case at a regular meeting of the board's trustees. Surveys of both teachers and parents will give added weight to opinions on the current state of in-school computers.

Working with IBM and Apple or other companies that have educational divisions, an energetic group could arrange a board-sponsored information night to bring teachers, principals, board members and the public together for a seminar, panel discussion and equipment displays which would attract community interest.

Parents need to follow school board politics closely and watch for opportunities to enter public debates. If trustees speak enthusiastically about joining the Internet, ask them whether the schools are already meeting provincial standards for computer education and whether the money and time spent exploring the net could not be better used to improve classroom resources or to introduce more basic technology, such as fax machines or voice mail.

Most important, throughout the process, do not be afraid to ask people to stop and explain more thoroughly what they are saying. Too many bureaucrats and trustees rely on pat answers and clichés to address problems, burying meaningful discussion in bafflegab. Don't be afraid to paraphrase your interpretation of their answers, and ask them to confirm your understanding. Always be ready to probe deeper to find out whether there is substance behind the talk.

Remember that provincial statutes set out the minimum standards for all education and that school boards are required to ensure their schools meet those standards. In theory, a school board can be made to answer to the province for its shortcomings, and the fear of a formal complaint against a board may, in the end, force some grudging improvement. But a threat at any level of the discussion should be a last resort, given the resistance it will induce.

Luckily, there is a spirit of enthusiasm for technological change wafting across Canada. In its 1995 report, Ontario's Royal Commission on Learning recommended that the Ontario government stop counting the number of computers in schools and start concentrating on the quality of learning and teaching technology. New Brunswick, too, emphasized the need for better facilities and equipment in its 1992 report "Excellence in Education," promising more money and higher standards for computers and online networking.

The mood for change is good, and it is up to parents to be sure that those government policies, both new and old, get translated into effective computer education at the classroom level.

Acknowledgments

The authors owe their gratitude to dozens of parents, teachers, administrators, computer enthusiasts, business executives — and even some kids — from across Canada who shared their thoughts, concerns and suggestions.

Special thanks go to Melanie Harris, Liz Paris, Neil Armitage, Roger Dixie, John Olson, Ruth Baumann, Michael Hiltz, Phil Hunt, John Spence, Bill Egnatoff, Larry Miller, Gerald Hurtubise, Jonathon Forbes, Brent Watson, the librarians at Queen's University, the members of the Educational Computing Organization of Ontario, the conference staff at the Information Technology Association of Canada and the networkers on America Online and The Well.

Extra-special assistance came from Susan Dickinson, Martin Waxman and cartoonist/co-publisher John Bianchi, who suggests that we stick to projects of fewer than 500 words from now on.